Hugo's Simplified

Japanese
Phrase Book

Hugo's Language Books Limited

Compiled by
Lexus Ltd
with
Keiko Holmes
and
Anthony P. Newell

5th impression 1992

Facts and figures given in this book were
correct when printed. If you discover any
changes, please write to us.

Set in 9/9 Plantin Light by
Typesetters Ltd and
printed in England by
Page Bros, Norwich

CONTENTS

PREFACE

This Japanese Phrase Book has the same excellent pedigree as all others in the Hugo series, having been compiled by experts to meet the general needs of tourists and business travellers, but it is - as you might expect - slightly different. Arranged under the usual headings of 'Hotels', 'Motoring' and so forth, the Japanese words and phrases you may need to use are printed in a modified version of the standard system of romanization - the way in which Japanese characters are written in our alphabet. After referring to the pronunciation notes you should have no difficulty reading these phrases straight off the page.

By omitting the traditional phrase book 'imitated pronunciation' (which would have taken up space without adding very much help in this instance) we have been able to give a far wider selection of *Things you'll see*. These recognition sections appear under each heading, and cover words, signs, notices etc.; the Japanese script is given alongside its romanized version and the English translation.

Also included is a special section covering business talk. There is a 2000-line mini-dictionary to help you form additional phrases (or at least express the one word you need!), and the extensive menu reader will ease your way through complicated Japanese meals. Under the heading *Cross-cultural Notes* you will find guidance on aspects of the Japanese way of life - points of etiquette, good manners and customs. An understanding of such matters will greatly enhance your trip to Japan, and your hosts will appreciate all the effort you have made to respect their culture and to speak their language.

PRONUNCIATION

When reading the imitated pronunciation, the same value should be given to all syllables as there is practically no stress in Japanese words (say 'Yo-ko-ha-ma' and not 'Yo-ko-HAR-ma'). Pronounce each syllable as if it formed part of an English word and you will be understood sufficiently well. Remember the points below and your pronunciation will be even closer to the correct Japanese.

a   as in 'Ma' but shorter
e   as in 'bed'
i   as the vowel sound in 'leaf' but shorter
o   as in 'more' but shorter
u   as in 'put'

A bar-line over a vowel means that the vowel should be spoken with twice the length of a single vowel.

When two vowels come together be careful to give each one its proper individual sound:

ai   as in 'wine'
ae   as if written 'mah-eh'
ei   as if written 'ay'

There are no silent letters, so don't forget to pronounce every one, including the 'e' at the end of a word (*mame* is pronounced as if written 'mah-meh').

g   is hard as in 'get'
j   as in 'jet'

If a 'p' or a 'k' or another consonant, apart from an 'n', comes at the end of a word, then it should be given its full value and not swallowed. Some systems write the word 'kip', for example, as 'kip-pu', which the authors of this book, however, consider likely to overemphasize the value of the final sound.

CROSS-CULTURAL NOTES

Superficially, Japan can seem very Westernized with all its American films, fast-food outlets and Western-style hotels. But old habits die hard, and in Japan tradition is still strong. With a little foreknowledge of Japanese customs and a modicum of effort to accommodate what may seem strange, the visitor to Japan will demonstrate a feeling of respect and goodwill towards the Japanese that will be amply rewarded.

When meeting a Japanese for the first time, both bowing and shaking hands are common (sometimes even together). Many Japanese are now used to hand-shaking, but if being introduced to someone out of reach, or to a group of people, bowing is simpler: just bend slightly forward from the waist, nod your head and smile.

Unless you are good friends, it is unusual to address a Japanese by his or her Christian name. Stick to the surname and add *-san* (an all-purpose word for Mr/Mrs/Ms). From the Western point of view Japanese names are written backwards – so, in *Tanaka Taro* 'Tanaka' is the surname and 'Taro' is the Christian name. The word *-san* can be added to Christian names as well as to surnames. But you should not use it when referring to yourself or when talking to members of your own family.

The Japanese see themselves as a more or less classless society. But status is important, and in the business world, for example, you will find a rigid hierarchy in operation. If you in any way offend Japanese sensibilities, apologize profusely.

If you are invited to a Japanese home, removal of shoes is a must. Slippers will be offered at the *genkan* or entrance. But even these must be left outside a room with *tatami* (straw matting). When you use the toilet you will usually find another pair of slippers awaiting you. Remember to change back out of your toilet slippers before re-entering the sitting room!

When entering a room you can say *ojama-shi-mass* which means literally 'I'm disturbing you', or *shitsurei-shi-mass* which means literally 'I'm being impolite'. The latter phrase can also be used when parting company.

Sometimes, when arriving at a Japanese home, you may be invited to take a bath. This is not a reflection of your host's opinion of your personal hygiene, but a courtesy offered to an honoured visitor to enable him to relax. Remember: the bath is for relaxing; the shower is for washing. The bathroom floor is tiled and it is on the floor that you wash yourself with soap and rinse off *before* stepping into the bath. The cardinal rule: don't get soap in the bathwater.

Some of the basic etiquette surrounding Japanese food and drink is:

● Be prepared to sit on cushions on the floor and use the damp flannel which will be offered to you to wipe your hands.

● Before eating you thank your host with *itadaki-mass* (literally 'I receive'), and when finished you again show your appreciation with *gochisō-sama deshta* (literally 'it was a feast').

● If you use chopsticks, never stand them upright in a bowl of rice (which is reminiscent of offerings to the dead) – if you want to let go of them, place them on the chopstick rest provided or lay them flat on a bowl or plate. Chopsticks will often come joined at one end – just split them apart. If dipping into a communal dish, it is polite to reverse the chopsticks and use the clean ends.

● Slurping noodles is quite acceptable.

● The way to eat soup is to hold the bowl to your mouth and drink; some people also eat rice by holding the bowl to the mouth and shovelling the rice in using chopsticks.

● Don't pour soy sauce over your rice – pour it over your meat instead or into your side dish.

● Don't pour your own *sake* – pour someone else's, who will then reciprocate by filling your cup, which ideally you should hold while the drink is being poured.

Although hotels, restaurants and department stores in big cities provide Western-style toilets, Japanese-style toilets are common (in trains, local inns and many houses, for example). There are different sorts of Japanese-style toilet, but what they all have in common is the fact that they are not to be sat on. The user squats over the receptacle, facing the hood at the far end. It is advisable to carry your own supply of tissue. Toilets are usually separate from bathrooms, so beware of asking for the bathroom if that's not exactly what you mean.

To the Japanese, the Western-style habit of blowing your nose into a handkerchief is an extremely distasteful practice. When you blow your nose, use a tissue. The Japanese use handkerchiefs for other purposes such as drying their hands when they have washed them after going to the toilet or as a napkin when at table.

If you see Japanese wearing face masks, this does not mean they are concerned about breathing *in* polluted air, but rather that they have a cold and are anxious not to breathe *out* germs.

Western women visiting Japan should not find their treatment noticeably different from what they are used to at home. But if you are in Japan on business, wives will be noticeably absent from a company's social activities. If you are lucky enough to be invited home, the wife will probably retire to the kitchen after serving dinner. It is, however, typical in Japan for the wife to control the family budget and for the husband to bring his pay-packet home and be given pocket money.

USEFUL EVERYDAY PHRASES

Yes/no
Hai/ie

Thank you
Dōmo arigatō

No thank you
Kek-kō dess arigatō

Please *(offering)* Dōzo
(asking for something) Onegai-shi-mass

I don't understand
Wakari-masen

Do you speak English?
Eigo o hanashi-mass ka?

I can't speak Japanese
Nihongo wa hanase-masen

I don't know
Shiri-masen

Please speak more slowly
Mō skoshi yuk-kuri hanashte kudasai

Please write it down for me
Kaite kure-masen ka?

My name is ...
Watashi no namae wa ... dess

How do you do, pleased to meet you
Hajime-mashte, dōzo yoroshku

Good morning
Ohayō gozai-mass

Good afternoon
Kon-nichi wa

Good evening
Kom-ban wa

Good night *(when going to bed)* Oyasumi nasai
   (when leaving a group early) Osaki ni

Goodbye
Sayonara

How are you?
Ogenki dess ka?

Excuse me please
Shitsurei shi-mass

Sorry!
Sumi-masen

I'm really sorry
Hontō ni sumi-masen

Can you help me?
Chot-to sumi-masen

Can you tell me ...?
... o oshiete kure-masen ka?

USEFUL EVERYDAY PHRASES

Can I have ...?
... itadake-mass ka?

I would like ...
... o itadake-mass ka?

Is there ... here?
Koko ni ... ga ari-mass ka?

Where can I get ...?
... wa doko ni ari-mass ka?

How much is it?
Ikura dess ka?

What time is it?
Ima nanji dess ka?

I must go now
Mō ikanakereba nari-masen

I've lost my way
Michi ni mayot-te shimai-mashta

Cheers!
Kampai!

Do you take credit cards?
Kurejit-to kādo tskae-mass ka?

Where is the toilet?
Otearai wa doko dess ka?

Go away!
At-chi e it-te!

Excellent!
Sugoi!

THINGS YOU'LL HEAR

Abunai!	Look out!
Chot-to!	Hey!
Dō itashi-mashte	You're welcome
Dōmo	Thanks
Dōzo	Here you are
E? Nan dess ka?	Pardon?
Genki dess, arigatō – anata wa?	Very well, thank you – and you?
Hajime-mashte, dōzo yoroshku	How do you do, nice to meet you
Ja mata	See you later
Ogenki dess ka?	How are you?
Sayonara	Goodbye
Sō dess	That's right
Sō dess ka?	Is that so?
Sumi-masen	Excuse me
Wakari-masen	I don't understand, I don't know

THINGS YOU'LL SEE

注意	**chūi**	caution
休日	**kyūjits**	closed
危険	**kiken**	danger
非常口	**hijō-guchi**	emergency exit
入口	**iriguchi**	entrance

⟶

出口	**deguchi**	exit
案内	**an-nai**	information
化粧室	**keshō-shits**	ladies
エレベーター	**erebētā**	lift
男子用	**danshi-yō**	(for) men
立入禁止	**tachi-iri-kinshi**	no admittance
禁煙	**kin-en**	no smoking
開く	**hirak**	open
営業中	**eigyō-chū**	open for business
故障	**koshō**	out of order
引く	**hik**	pull
押す	**oss**	push
閉じる	**tojiru**	shut
階	**-kai**	storey, floor
御手洗	**otearai**	toilet
女子用	**joshi-yō**	(for) women
円	**en**	yen

DAYS, MONTHS, SEASONS

Sunday	nichi-yōbi
Monday	getsu-yōbi
Tuesday	ka-yōbi
Wednesday	sui-yōbi
Thursday	moku-yōbi
Friday	kin-yōbi
Saturday	do-yōbi
January	ichi-gats
February	ni-gats
March	san-gats
April	shi-gats
May	go-gats
June	roku-gats
July	shchi-gats
August	hachi-gats
September	ku-gats
October	jū-gats
November	jū-ichi-gats
December	jū-ni-gats
Spring	haru
Summer	nats
Autumn	aki
Winter	huyu
Christmas	kuriss-mass
Christmas Eve	kuriss-mass ibu
New Year	oshō-gats
New Year's Eve	ō-misoka

THE CALENDAR

1st	tsuitachi
2nd	hutska
3rd	mik-ka
4th	yok-ka
5th	itska
6th	muika
7th	nanoka
8th	yōka
9th	kokonoka
10th	tōka
11th	jū-ichi-nichi
12th	jū-ni-nichi
13th	jū-san-nichi
14th	jū-yok-ka
15th	jū-go-nichi
16th	jū-roku-nichi
17th	jū-nana-nichi
18th	jū-hachi-nichi
19th	jū-ku-nichi
20th	hatska
21st	ni-jū-ichi-nichi
22nd	ni-jū-ni-nichi
23rd	ni-jū-san-nichi
24th	ni-jū-yok-ka
25th	ni-jū-go-nichi
26th	ni-jū-roku-nichi
27th	ni-jū-nana-nichi
28th	ni-jū-hachi-nichi
29th	ni-jū-ku-nichi
30th	san-jū-nichi
31st	san-jū-ichi-nichi

NUMBERS

0	zero	○	**10**	jū	十
1	ichi	一	**11**	jū-ichi	十一
2	ni	二	**12**	jū-ni	十二
3	san	三	**13**	jū-san	十三
4	yon	四	**14**	jū-yon	十四
5	go	五	**15**	jū-go	十五
6	roku	六	**16**	jū-roku	十六
7	nana	七	**17**	jū-nana	十七
8	hachi	八	**18**	jū-hachi	十八
9	kyū	九	**19**	jū-kyū	十九

20	ni-jū	二十
21	ni-jū-ichi	二十一
22	ni-jū-ni	二十二
30	san-jū	三十
40	yon-jū	四十
50	go-jū	五十
60	roku-jū	六十
70	nana-jū	七十
80	hachi-jū	八十
90	kyū-jū	九十

NUMBERS

100	hyaku	百
101	hyaku-ichi	百一
200	ni-hyaku	二百
300	sam-byaku	三百
400	yon-hyaku	四百
500	go-hyaku	五百
600	rop-pyaku	六百
700	nana-hyaku	七百
800	hap-pyaku	八百
900	kyū-hyaku	九百
1000	sen	千
2000	ni-sen	二千
3000	san-zen	三千
4000	yon-sen	四千
5000	go-sen	五千
6000	rok-sen	六千
7000	nana-sen	七千
8000	hass-sen	八千
9000	kyū-sen	九千
10,000	ichi-man	一万
20,000	ni-man	二万
100,000	jū-man	十万
200,000	ni-jū-man	二十万

1,000,000	hyaku-man	百万
2,000,000	ni-hyaku-man	二百万
10,000,000	sem-man	千万
20,000,000	ni-sem-man	二千万
100,000,000	ichi-ok	一億
123,456	jū-ni-man-san-zen-yon-hyaku-go-jū-rok	十二万三千四百五十六

COUNTING

When counting **objects** Japanese has different number words. Note that the number comes after the object.

two beers   bı̄ru hutats

one	hitots
two	hutats
three	mits
four	yots
five	itsuts
six	muts
seven	nanats
eight	yats
nine	kokonots
ten	tō

After ten, use the ordinary number words again. For counting **people** there are two special points to note:

one person	hito-ri
two people	huta-ri

After this, use 'nin' with the ordinary number word:

three people	san-nin
ten people	jū-nin

TIME

today	kyō
yesterday	kinō
tomorrow	ashta
the day before yesterday	ototoi
the day after tomorrow	asat-te
this week	kon-shū
last week	sen-shū
next week	rai-shū
this morning	kesa
this afternoon	kyō no gogo
this evening	kom-ban
tonight	kon-ya
yesterday afternoon	kinō no gogo
last night	yūbe
tomorrow morning	ashta no asa
tomorrow night	ashta no ban
in three days	mik-ka go
three days ago	mik-ka mae
late	osoi
early	hayai
soon	sugu
later on	ato de
at the moment	ima
second	byō
minute	hun
one minute	ip-pun
two minutes	ni-hun
quarter of an hour	jū-go hun
half an hour	san-jup-pun
three quarters of an hour	yon-jū-go-hun
hour	jikan
that day	sono hi
every day	mainichi
all day	ichi-nichi jū

the next day	sono yokujits ni
week *(this, last, next etc)*	-shū
(one, two, three etc)	shū-kan
fortnight	ni-shū-kan
month *(this, last, next etc)*	gets
(one, two, three etc)	kagets
this year	kotoshi
last year	kyonen
next year	rainen
one year	ichi-nen

TELLING THE TIME

In Japanese the hour comes first, followed by the minutes. If the minutes are 'past' the hour, then just say the hour followed by the minutes as when saying 'five forty' or 'six ten'. So 'five past two' is *ni-ji go-hun*. *Ji* means 'hours' and *hun* means 'minutes'. If the minutes are 'before' the hour, then the number of minutes plus *mae* (before) is used. So 'five to three' is *san-ji go-hun mae*. The word for 'half' is *han*, which is simply added to the hour (e.g. 'half past three' is *san-ji han*). There is no special word for a quarter of an hour – just use 15 minutes *(jū-go hun)*. Timetables and other official lists use the 24-hour clock written in Arabic numerals.

am/pm	gozen/gogo
one o'clock	ichi-ji
ten past one	ichi-ji jup-pun
quarter past one	ichi-ji jū-go-hun
half past one	ichi-ji han
twenty to two	ni-ji ni-jup-pun mae
quarter to two	ni-ji jū-go-hun mae
two o'clock	ni-ji
16.30	jū-roku-ji san-jup-pun
at half past five	go-ji han ni
at seven o'clock	shchi-ji ni
noon	shōgo
midnight	mayonaka

HOTELS

Advance reservations are generally recommended and can be made through the JTB (Japanese Travel Bureau), whose offices can be found throughout Japan. There are two principal types of accommodation: Western-style hotels, *hoteru* and Japanese-style inns, *ryokan*.

Hotels are comparable in range, cost and quality with modern hotels in Britain and Europe. Facilities and services are good, though the rooms are often smaller than their Western counterparts. Vending machines are installed in most hotels for snacks, drinks and certain basic items. Tipping is generally unnecessary (the exception being, perhaps, baggage porters) as a service charge of 10-15% will be levied. In addition a 10% tax may be imposed, but only on bills exceeding a certain amount.

There are also what are known as 'business hotels' or *bijiness hoteru*. These are found in urban centres and are aimed primarily at the travelling businessman on a restricted budget. They are consequently very plain and offer a minimum service.

Motels are relatively cheap, but it should be borne in mind that some motels are used as 'love hotels'.

Ryokan, which offer the traveller a real taste of the traditional Japanese life-style, are becoming increasingly popular among tourists. Staying at a *ryokan* is not necessarily cheaper than staying at a hotel, but the service is invariably excellent and the room charge customarily includes breakfast and dinner. Guests live on traditional *tatami* matting, sleep in *futon* – Japanese bedding laid on the floor – eat Japanese cuisine and can relax in a piping hot communal Japanese bath. The public bathrooms are generally single sex, though there are still *ryokan* where men and women bathe together, particularly in the hot spring resorts of northern Japan, where people go expressly for the supposed therapeutic properties of the water. A number of *ryokan* have facilities for catering for Western visitors, providing, for example, individual bathrooms for those Westerners of a shy disposition. Unlike the staff of Western-style hotels, those who run *ryokan* generally speak little or no English.

Four other types of accommodation are available:

Youth Hostels: Simple, neat, inexpensive and usually well-sited, Japan's plentiful youth hostels are governed by the international rules of youth hostelling. A few are open to people of all ages, but many will require tourists to be members of their own national associations.

Minshku: Privately owned establishments, these are often run as sidelines by families who want to supplement their regular income, and are the nearest Japanese equivalent to the British bed and breakfast system. Rooms are simple (e.g. no luxury items like a refrigerator), the rates are very reasonable and staying in a *minshku* will give you a good chance to try some real Japanese home cooking. Reservations (plus deposits) are required a month in advance.

Kokumin Shkusha (People's lodges): Allowing people a chance to enjoy inexpensive holiday accommodation in pleasant surroundings, these facilities are basically set up to meet the requirements of Japanese travellers on limited budgets. They bear a certain resemblance to rural *ryokan* but are bigger and cheaper. Located as they are away from urban centres they are intended for vacationers rather than business people. As in the *ryokan* little or no English can be expected.

Kokumin Kyūka-mura (National vacation villages): These are health resorts set in beautiful surroundings; there are facilities for outdoor recreation in addition to the inexpensive accommodation; foreign visitors will be expected to adopt a Japanese-style life.

USEFUL WORDS AND PHRASES

balcony	barukonǐ
bathroom	ohuroba
bed	bed-do
bedroom	heya
bill	seikyū-sho
breakfast	chōshok
dining room	shoku-dō
dinner	yūshok
double room	daburu
foyer	robǐ

full board	san-shoku-tski
half board	chōshok to yūshoku-tski
hotel	hoteru
key	kagi
lift	erebētā
lounge	raunji
lunch	chūshok
manager	manējā
reception	huronto
receptionist	huronto no hito
restaurant	restoran
room	heya
room service	rūm-sābiss
shower	shawā
single room	shinguru
toilet	otearai
twin room	tsuin

Have you any vacancies?
Heya ga ari-mass ka?

I have a reservation
Yoyak shte i-mass

I'd like a single room
Shinguru onegai-shi-mass

I'd like a double room
Daburu onegai-shi-mass

I'd like a twin room
Tsuin onegai-shi-mass

I'd like a room with a bathroom
Ohuro-tski no heya onegai-shi-mass

I'd like a room with a balcony
Barukoni-tski no heya onegai-shi-mass

I'd like a room for one night
Ip-pak tomaritain dess

I'd like a room for three nights
Sam-pak tomaritain dess

What is the charge per night?
Ip-paku ikura dess ka?

I don't know yet how long I'll stay
Nan-nichi tomaru ka mada wakari-masen

When is breakfast?
Chōshoku wa nanji dess ka?

When is dinner?
Yūshoku wa nanji dess ka?

Would you have my luggage brought up?
Nimotsu o mot-te kite kure-masen ka?

Please call me at ... o'clock
... ji ni okoshte kudasai

Can I have breakfast in my room?
Heya de chōshoku ga deki-mass ka?

I'll be back at ... o'clock
... ji ni modori-mass

My room number is ...
Watashi no heya wa ... ban dess

I'm leaving tomorrow
Ashta tachi-mass

Can I have the bill please?
Seikyū-sho onegai-shi-mass

HOTELS

I'll pay by credit card
Kurejit-to kādo de harai-mass

I'll pay cash
Genkin de harai-mass

Can you get me a taxi?
Takshi o yonde kure-masen ka?

Can you recommend another hotel?
Hoka ni ī hoteru ga ari-mass ka?

THINGS YOU'LL HEAR

Mōshi-wake gozai-masen ga ip-pai dess
I'm sorry, we're full

Shinguru wa husagat-te ori-mass
There are no single rooms left

Daburu wa husagat-te ori-mass
There are no double rooms left

Nam-paku dess ka?
For how many nights?

Oshi-harai wa dō nasai-mass ka?
How will you be paying?

Saki-barai de onegai-itashi-mass
Please pay in advance

Kono kādo ni kinyū shte itadake-mass ka?
Could you fill in this registration form please?

Koko ni sain shte kudasai-mase
Sign here please

Paspōto, omochi dess ka?
May I see your passport?

THINGS YOU'LL SEE

バー	**bā**	bar
お風呂	**ohuro**	bath
冷房	**reibō**	air-conditioning
食堂	**shokudō**	dining room
ダイニング・ルーム	**dainin-gu rūm**	dining room
飲み水	**nomi-mizu**	drinking water
飲料水	**inryō-sui**	drinking water
クリーニング	**kurīnin-gu**	dry cleaning
エレベーター	**erebētā**	elevator
非常口	**hijō-guchi**	emergency exit
消火器	**shōkaki**	fire extinguisher
二階	**ni-kai**	first floor
一階	**ik-kai**	ground floor
暖房	**dambō**	heating

→

27

温泉	**onsen**	hot spring
ホテル	**hoteru**	hotel
日本交通公社	**Nihon kōtsū kōsha**	Japan Travel Bureau
旅館	**ryokan**	Japanese-style inn
和室	**washits**	Japanese-style room
ロビー	**robi̇̄**	lobby
ラウンジ	**raunji**	lounge
男	**otoko**	men
立入禁止	**tachi-iri-kinshi**	no entry
民宿	**minshku**	people's inn
受付	**uketske**	reception
フロント	**huronto**	reception
レストラン	**restoran**	restaurant
室	**heya**	room
ルーム・サービス	**rūm sābiss**	room service
お手洗い	**otearai**	toilet
自動販売器	**jidō-hambai-ki**	vending machine
洋室	**yōshits**	Western-style room
女	**on-na**	women
ユース・ホステル	**yūss-hosteru**	youth hostel

MOTORING

There are plenty of car hire companies in Japan and comprehensive insurance is usually included in the hire charge. To hire a car you will need an international driving licence. In Japan they drive on the LEFT and road signs often follow international conventions, although those giving names or information will be in Japanese. Petrol is bought by the litre, and you may find that filling stations will also do certain minor repairs. A red triangle is essential and should be provided by the hire company. The JAF (Japan Automobile Federation) offers free assistance to foreigners in case of breakdown or emergency. Expressways or motorways are good, but many ordinary roads are narrow and bumpy. In Japan you'll find that the roads are invariably overcrowded, a problem which is made worse by the lack of pavements, numerous level crossings, lack of parking space and ubiquitous electricity poles. All in all, driving in Japan can be a hazardous and frustrating experience.

USEFUL WORDS AND PHRASES

automatic	ōto
boot	torank
breakdown	koshō
brake	burēki
car	kuruma
clutch	kurachi
crossroads	jū-ji-ro
to drive	unten suru
engine	enjin
exhaust	haiki-gass
fanbelt	fam-beruto
garage *(for repairs)*	shūri-jō
(for petrol)	gasorin-stando
gear(s)	giya
junction (on motorway)	intā

licence	menkyo
lights *(head)*	hed-do-raito
(rear)	tēru-raito
lorry	torak
manual (drive)	shudō
mirror	bak-mirā
motorbike	ōtobai
motorway	kōsok-dōro
number plate	nambā-purēto
petrol	gasorin
road	michi
to skid	suberu
spares	speya
speed	sokudo
speed limit	sokudo-seigen
speedometer	sokudo-kei
steering wheel	handoru
to tow	hik
traffic lights	shingō
trailer	torērā
tyre	taiya
van	ban
wheel	sharin
windscreen	uindo-skrīn
windscreen wiper	uindo-skrīn waipā

I'd like some petrol/oil/water
Gasorin/oiru/mizu onegai-shi-mass

Fill her up please!
Mantan onegai-shi-mass

I'd like 10 litres of petrol
Gasorin jū-rit-toru onegai-shi-mass

Would you check the tyres please?
Taiya o mite kure-masen ka?

Do you do repairs?
Shūri shte kure-masen ka?

Can you repair the clutch?
Kurachi naoshte kure-masen ka?

How long will it take?
Dono kurai kakari-mass ka?

Where can I park?
Doko ni chūsha deki-mass ka?

Can I park here?
Koko ni chūsha shte mo ī dess ka?

There is something wrong with the engine
Enjin ga dōka shi-mashta

The engine is overheating
Enjin ga obāhīto shi-mashta

I need a new tyre
Atarashī taiya ga iri-mass

I'd like to hire a car
Kuruma o karitai to omoi-mass

Is there a mileage charge?
Kyori de harai-mass ka?

Where is the nearest garage?
Ichiban chikai garēji wa doko dess ka?

How do I get to ...?
... e, dō ikeba īn dess ka?

Is this the road to ...?
Kore ga ... e iku michi dess ka?

31

DIRECTIONS YOU MAY BE GIVEN

mass-sugu	straight on
hidari ni	on the left
hidari ni magat-te	turn left
migi ni	on the right
migi ni magat-te	turn right
migi-gawa no saisho no michi	first on the right
hidari-gawa no nibam-me no michi	second on the left
... o tōt-te	past the ...

THINGS YOU'LL HEAR

Ōtomachik ga ī dess ka, shudō ga ī dess ka?
Would you like an automatic or a manual?

Menkyo-shō o misete kudasai
May I see your licence?

SOME COMMON ROAD SIGNS

この先 100 メートル	**kono saki hyaku mētoru**	100 metres ahead
この先 100 米	**kono saki hyaku mētoru**	100 metres ahead
駐車場	**chūsha-jō**	car park
満車	**man-sha**	car park full
回り道	**mawari-michi**	diversion

非常駐車帯	**hijō chūsha-tai**	emergency parking area
出口	**deguchi**	exit
高速道路	**kōsok dōro**	expressway
交差点	**kōsaten**	junction
本線	**honsen**	lane for through traffic
踏切	**humi-kiri**	level crossing
最高速度	**saikō sokudo**	maximum speed
国道	**kokudō**	national motorway
左折禁止	**sasets kinshi**	no left turn
駐車禁止	**chūsha kinshi**	no parking
右折禁止	**usets kinshi**	no right turn
停車禁止	**teisha kinshi**	no stopping
通行止	**tsūkō-dome**	no through traffic
通行禁止	**tsūkō-kinshi**	no through traffic
スピード落せ	**spīdo otose**	reduce speed
道路工事	**dōro-kōji**	road under construction
工事中	**kōji-chū**	road works
急カーブ	**kyū-kāb**	sharp bend
一時預り	**ichiji azukari**	short-term parking

→

33

徐行	**jokō**	slow
止まれ	**tomare**	stop
一旦停車	**it-tan tei-sha**	stop
一旦停止	**it-tan tei shi**	stop
有料道路	**yū-ryō dōro**	toll road
事故	**jiko**	accident
自動車整備工場	**jidōsha seibi kōjō**	auto repairs
料金	**ryōkin**	charge
灯油	**tōyu**	paraffin
有料	**yū-ryō**	pay to park here
無料	**mu-ryō**	no charge
石油	**sekiyu**	petrol
ガソリンスタンド	**gasorin stando**	petrol station
警察	**keisats**	police

RAIL TRAVEL

Japan runs a very efficient train system which is fast and punctual. Large stations offer all the usual services, including baggage porters (called *akabō* because of their red caps). First class coaches, 'green cars', with a green four-leaf clover symbol on the side of the coach, offer roomy and comfortable reclining seats. Second class coaches are often crowded. Station names and important signs are given in both Japanese and English, though verbal announcements are always made in Japanese – except on the 'bullet train'.

There are various categories of train:

● *Shinkansen:* this is the 'bullet train', one of the world's fastest luxury trains; there are two types – the *hikari* and the *kodama*; the *kodama* stops at more stations and therefore takes slightly longer to arrive.

● *Tok-kyū:* the special express which stops only at main stations.

● *Kyūkō:* the express, stopping more frequently than the *tok-kyū*.

● *Hutsū:* the local train which stops at all stations.

There are plenty of automatic ticket vending machines, but if in doubt you can always go to the ticket office. For the faster trains you pay an express surcharge; there is a further charge for reservations – but this is usually worthwhile since many trains are crowded.

USEFUL WORDS AND PHRASES

booking office	kip-pu uriba
buffet	byuf-fe
carriage	kyak-sha
compartment	sha-shits
communication cord	hijō-tsūhō-sak
connection	norikae
dining car	shokudō-sha
engine	enjin
entrance	iriguchi
exit	deguchi

first class	it-tō
to get in	noru
to get out	oriru
guard	shashō
indicator board	hyōji-ban
left luggage (office)	tenimotsu azukari-jo
lost property	wasure-mono
luggage rack	nidai
luggage trolley	te-oshi-guruma
luggage van	nimots-sha
platform	hōm
rail	rēru
railway	tetsudō
reserved seat	shtei-seki
restaurant car	shokudō-sha
return ticket	ōhuku kip
seat	seki
second class	ni-tō
single ticket	katamichi kip
sleeping car	shindai-sha
station	eki
station master	eki-chō
ticket	kip
ticket collector	eki-in
timetable	jikok-hyō
tracks	rēru
train	densha
waiting room	machi-ai-shits
window	mado

When does the train for ... leave?
... iki no densha wa nanji ni de-mass ka?

When does the train from ... arrive?
... kara no densha wa nanji ni tski-mass ka?

When is the next train to ... ?
... iki no tsugi no densha wa nanji dess ka?

When is the first train to ...?
... iki no saisho no densha wa nanji dess ka?

When is the last train to ...?
... iki no saigo no densha wa nanji dess ka?

What is the fare to ...?
... made ikura dess ka?

Do I have to change?
Norikae nakereba nari-masen ka?

Does the train stop at ...?
Densha wa ... ni tomari-mass ka?

How long does it take to get to ...?
... made dono gurai kakari-mass ka?

A single/return ticket to ... please
... made katamichi/ōhuku ichi-mai onegai-shi-mass

Do I have to pay a supplement?
Tsuika-kin o harawa-nakereba nari-masen ka?

I'd like to reserve a seat
Seki o yoyak shtain dess

Is this the right train for ...?
... e wa kono densha de īn dess ka?

Is this the right platform for the ... train?
... densha wa kono hōm de īn dess ka?

Which platform for the ... train?
... densha wa dono hōm dess ka?

Is the train late?
Densha wa okurete-i-mass ka?

Could you help me with my luggage please?
Nimotsu o mot-te kure-masen ka?

Is this a non-smoking compartment?
Kore wa kin-en-sha dess ka?

Is this seat free?
Kono seki wa aite-i-mass ka?

This seat is taken
Kono seki wa aite-i-masen

I have reserved this seat
Kono seki o yoyak shte-i-mass

May I open the window?
Mado o akete mo ī dess ka?

May I close the window?
Mado o shimete mo ī dess ka?

When do we arrive in …?
… ni nanji ni tski-mass ka?

What station is this?
Kono eki wa doko dess ka?

Do we stop at …?
… ni tomari-mass ka?

Would you keep an eye on my things for a moment?
Chot-to kore o mite-ite kure-masen ka?

Is there a restaurant car on this train?
Kono densha ni shokudō-sha ga ari-mass ka?

THINGS YOU'LL HEAR

Gorenraku itashi-mass
Attention

Kip-pu o haiken sasete itadaki-mass
Tickets please

Chot-to sumi-masen!
Excuse me!

Ori-mass!
I'm getting off!

Tsumete kudasai!
Move along please!

THINGS YOU'LL SEE

特急	**tok-kyū**	(abbreviation for) limited express
大人	**otona**	adult
前売券	**mae-uri-ken**	advance sale tickets
下車前途無効	**gesha zento mukō**	after alighting, not valid for further travel
到着	**tōchak**	arrival(s)
のりば・乗り場	**noriba**	boarding platform

→

回数券	**kaisū-ken**	book of tickets
…行き	**… yuki**	bound for …
新幹線	**shinkan-sen**	bullet train
三号車	**san-gō-sha**	car no. 3
小人・子供	**kodomo**	child
出発	**shup-pats**	departure(s)
発車	**hash-sha**	departure(s)
行先	**yuki-saki**	destination
食堂車	**shokudō-sha**	dining car
方面	**hōmen**	direction
東口	**higashi guchi**	east exit
精算所	**seisan-jo**	excess fare office
急行	**kyūkō**	express
一等	**it-tō**	first class
みどりの窓口	**midori-no-madoguchi**	first class ticket window
200 円区間ゆき	**ni-hyaku-en kukan yuki**	for destinations within the 200-yen zone
グリーン車	**gurǐn-sha**	green car
団体	**dantai**	group
車掌	**shashō**	guard

個人	**kojin**	individual
国鉄	**koktets**	Japan National Railways (JNR)
左側通行	**hidari gawa tsūkō**	keep to the left
右側通行	**migi gawa tsūkō**	keep to the right
売店	**baiten**	kiosk
コインロッカー	**koin rok-kā**	left luggage locker
一時預り所	**ichiji-azukari-jo**	left luggage office
特別急行	**tokubets-kyūkō**	limited express
…線	**…sen**	… line
お忘れもの	**owasure-mono**	lost property
お忘れもの承り所	**owasure-mono uketa-mawari-jo**	lost property office
遺失物取扱所	**ishits-buts tori-atskai-jo**	lost property office
荷物	**nimots**	luggage
地図	**chizu**	map
次	**tsugi**	next
北口	**kita guchi**	north exit
無効	**mukō**	not valid
普通	**hutsū**	ordinary

→

ホーム	**hōm**	platform
入場券	**nyū-jō-ken**	platform ticket
私鉄	**shitets**	private railways
鉄道	**tetsudō**	railway
指定席（券）	**shtei-seki (-ken)**	reserved seat (ticket)
定期券	**teiki-ken**	season ticket
席	**seki**	seat
座席	**zaseki**	seat
二等	**ni-tō**	second class
準急	**jun-kyū**	semi-express
南口	**minami guchi**	south exit
駅	**eki**	station
駅長	**eki-chō**	station master
料金表	**ryōkin-hyō**	table of charges
運賃表	**unchin-hyō**	table of fares
乗換口	**nori-kae-guchi**	this way for changing trains
切符	**kip**	ticket
…券	**…-ken**	… ticket
改札口	**kai-sats guchi**	ticket barrier
きっぷうりば 切符売場	**kip-pu uriba**	ticket office/ machine

窓口	**madoguchi**	ticket window
出札口	**shuss-sats-guchi**	ticket window
時刻表	**jikok-hyō**	timetable
二番線	**ni-ban-sen**	track no. 2
電車	**densha**	train
列車	**resh-sha**	train
地下鉄	**chikatets**	underground
自由席	**ji-yū-seki**	unreserved seat
有効	**yūkō**	valid
発売当日限り有効	**hatsubai tōjits kagiri yūkō**	valid only on day of purchase
経由	**keiyu**	via
待合室	**machi-ai-shits**	waiting room
西口	**nishi guchi**	west exit

AIR TRAVEL

Enquiries should be made at the Japanese embassy in the country of departure for details on visas, customs formalities and vaccination requirements. This done, entry formalities can be kept to a minimum, requiring the filling-in of a disembarkation form on the plane, a stamp in your passport from the immigration officer and perhaps a *nani mo arimasen* – 'I have nothing (to declare)' – from you to the customs officer. Many airport officials can speak at least some English, and all major airports have very good information centres staffed by English-speakers.

USEFUL WORDS AND PHRASES

aircraft	hikōki
air hostess	schūwādess
airline	kōkū
airport	kūkō
airport bus	eyapōto bass
aisle	tsūro
arrival	tōchak
baggage claim	onimotsu uketori-jo
boarding card	tōjō-ken
check-in	chek-ku-in
check-in desk	chek-ku-in kauntā
customs	zeikan
delay	okure
departure	shup-pats
departure lounge	shup-pats raunji
emergency exit	hijō guchi
flight	hikō
flight number	huraito bangō
gate	gēto
jet	jet-to
to land	chaku-rik suru

long distance flight	chōkyori bin
passport	paspōto
passport control	nyūkok shinsa
pilot	pairot-to
runway	kass-sō-ro
seat	seki
seat belt	shīto-beruto
steward	schūwādo
stewardess	schūwādess
take-off	ririk
window	mado
wing	tsubasa

When is there a flight to ...?
... iki no huraito wa its dess ka?

What time does the flight to ... leave?
... iki no huraito wa nanji ni shup-pats shi-mass ka?

Is it a direct flight?
Chok-kō-bin dess ka?

Do I have to change planes?
Norikae nakereba nari-masen ka?

When do I have to check in?
Chek-ku-in wa nanji dess ka?

I'd like a single ticket to ...
... iki no katamichi onegai-shi-mass

I'd like a return ticket to ...
... iki no ōhuku onegai-shi-mass

I'd like a non-smoking seat please
Kin-en shitsu onegai-shi-mass

I'd like a smoking seat please
Kitsuen no hō onegai-shi-mass

I'd like a window seat please
Madogawa onegai-shi-mass

How long will the flight be delayed?
Hikōki wa dono kurai okure-mass ka?

Is this the right gate for the ... flight?
... iki no huraito no gēto wa koko dess ka?

Which gate for the flight to ...?
... iki no huraito no gēto wa doko dess ka?

When do we arrive in ...?
... e nanji ni tski-mass ka?

May I smoke now?
Ima tabako o sut-te mo ī dess ka?

I do not feel very well
Kibun ga yoku ari-masen

THINGS YOU'LL HEAR

Tadaima kara ... bin no tōjō tetsuzuki o hajime-mass
The flight for ... is now boarding

... ban gēto ni onarabi kudasai
Please go now to gate number ...

THINGS YOU'LL SEE

航空	**kōkū**	airline
航空券	**kōkū-ken**	airline ticket
空港	**kūkō**	airport
全日空	**Zen Nik-kū**	All Nippon Airways
到着	**tōchak**	arrivals
搭乗口	**tōjō-guchi**	gate
搭乗券	**tōjō-ken**	boarding pass
バス	**bass**	buses
税関	**zeikan**	customs
出発	**shup-pats**	departures
国内線	**kokunai-sen**	domestic airlines
免税店	**menzei-ten**	duty-free shop
ゲート	**gēto**	gate
出入国管理	**shuts-nyū-goku kanri**	immigration
御案内所	**go-an-nai sho**	information desk
国際線	**koksai-sen**	international airlines
日本航空	**Nihon Kōkū**	Japan Airlines
予約	**yoyak**	reservations
タクシー	**takshī**	taxis
東亜国内航空	**Tōa Kokunai Kōkū**	TOA Domestic Airlines

BY BUS, TAXI AND UNDERGROUND

Buses abound, but in the rush hour they are slow and overcrowded. In general they are less convenient than trains unless you know where to get off. Different systems operate – sometimes you board at the front and exit at the rear; sometimes it's the other way round. Sometimes you pay for the distance travelled; sometimes there is a flat fare. Whatever the fare is, you usually drop it into the 'fare box' or *ryōkim-bako* rather than hand it to the driver. No English can be expected from either bus signs or bus drivers.

Taxis can be flagged down in the street (a red light indicating an available cab) or queued for at a taxi rank, *takshī noriba*. Try to have the address you want to go to written down in Japanese. Preferably this should be accompanied by a map as addresses in Japan are notoriously difficult to find. Many streets have no name and the numbering system has a form of logic unique to Japan. For the return trip just hand the driver one of your hotel's business cards (available at the front desk). Always get in and out of the taxi on the left – and don't try to open the door by yourself: this is done automatically by a gadget operated by the driver. A late night surcharge is payable between 11.00pm and 5.00am. Tipping is not required.

There are undergrounds, *chikatets*, in large cities like Tokyo, Osaka, Kyoto and Sapporo. With the dense congestion on Japan's roads, the underground is often the fastest and most reliable means of transport. Fares depend on distance travelled and tickets are most conveniently obtained from vending machines (which also give change). During the rush hour stations both above and below ground are only for those of a strong and healthy disposition.

Other means of transport: there are many ferries around Japan, plus a few trams in big cities (though these are fast disappearing). There is a monorail from downtown Tokyo to Haneda Airport. Ask for details at a JTB office. Do not expect to find rickshaws.

USEFUL WORDS AND PHRASES

adult   otona

boat	bōto
bus	bass
bus stop	bass-tei
child	kodomo
coach	chōkyori-bass
connection	norikae
driver	untenshu
fare	ryōkin
ferry	ferī
lake	mizu-umi
network map	chizu
number 5 bus	go-ban no bass
passenger	jōkyak
port	minato
river	kawa
rush hour	rash-shu-awā
seat	seki
station	eki
subway	chikadō
taxi	takshī
terminus	shūten
ticket	kip
tram	shigai-densha
underground	chikatets

Where is the nearest underground station?
Moyori no chikatets no eki wa doko dess ka?

Where is the bus station?
Bass no eki wa doko dess ka?

Where is there a bus stop?
Bass-tei wa doko dess ka?

Which buses go to ...?
Dono bass ga ... e iki-mass ka?

BY BUS, TAXI AND UNDERGROUND

How often do the buses to ... run?
... iki no bass wa ichi-jikan ni nambon ari-mass ka?

Would you tell me when we get to ...?
... ni tsuitara oshiete kure-masen ka?

Do I have to get off yet?
Mada ori-naktemo in dess ka?

How do you get to ...?
... e wa dō iki-mass ka?

Is it very far?
Totemo tōi dess ka?

I want to go to ...
... e ikitai to omoi-mass

Do you go near ...?
... no chikaku e iki-mass ka?

Where can I buy a ticket?
Doko de kip ga kae-mass ka?

Could you close the window?
Mado o shimete kure-masen ka?

Could you open the window?
Mado o akete kure-masen ka?

Could you help me get a ticket?
Kip-pu o kau no o tetsudat-te kure-masen ka?

When does the last bus leave?
Saishū bass wa nanji de-mass ka?

THINGS YOU'LL SEE

自動ドア	**jidō-doa**	automatic door
バス	**bass**	bus
バス乗り場	**bass-noriba**	bus boarding point
バス停	**bass-tei**	bus stop
バスターミナル	**bass-tāminaru**	bus terminal
乗車は前扉から	**jōsha wa mae-tobira kara**	enter at front door
降車は後扉から	**kōsha wa ushiro-tobira kara**	exit at rear door
料金箱	**ryōkim-bako**	fare box
運賃箱	**unchim-bako**	fare box
料金メーター	**ryōkin-mētā**	fare meter
空車	**kūsha**	for hire
駅前	**eki-mae**	in front of station
夜間割増し料金	**yakan warimashi ryōkin**	late night fare
回送	**kaisō**	out of service
次停車	**tsugi teisha**	stopping at next stop
タクシー	**takshǐ**	taxi
タクシー乗り場	**takshǐ-noriba**	taxi rank
地下鉄	**chikatets**	underground

DOING BUSINESS

The stereotyped image of the British businessman as held by the Japanese is of someone who dresses sloppily, stays in the cheapest possible hotel, is late for appointments and is completely ignorant of Japanese customs. As a foreign visitor you will undoubtedly be shown respect, but if you avoid falling into the stereotype this respect will be more than superficial.

Position within a hierarchy is important to the Japanese. Your business card, which is a crucial item to take, should state what your own position is within your own company, otherwise the Japanese will be confused. Foreign businessmen often make the mistake of addressing the wrong level of authority within a Japanese company. Key figures will be the *buchō* (department or division chief) and the *kachō* (section chief). The *kachō* makes all the routine business decisions and supervises their implementation. Do not attempt to by-pass such people and go straight to the top.

The foreign businessman looking for a quick decision will most likely be frustrated in Japan. A key concept in Japanese business is that of *nemawashi* - the groundwork prior to decision-making involving enlisting the support of all those concerned in the decision-making process. It should also be appreciated that the Japanese approach to a business decision is less along the lines of 'what's in it for us?' or 'what's the profit?' than 'what are we getting ourselves into?'. Strategic issues of market share tend to override tactical considerations of quick profit. First meetings should be seen as an occasion for establishing 'face' and for triggering groundwork.

Although Japanese men do not generally regard women as equals, foreign businesswomen will be given 'honorary male' status.

Here are some general tips that might make your trip more successful:

It is a good idea to take small gifts for your Japanese business partners. If you are taken out for a meal, do not insist on paying. Bowing is no longer essential in Japan - shaking hands is quite acceptable. Learn something about Japanese customs (see page 7). Learn some facts about Japan: the names of the Prime Minister and Foreign

Minister, the names of the Governor of the Bank of Japan and the President of the company you're dealing with, even the names of some film stars or sporting heroes. In other words, show some interest in and knowledge of Japan. Those who ignore such basics will find themselves in Japan climbing not just a hill but a very steep mountain.

USEFUL WORDS AND PHRASES

accept	shōdak suru
accountant	keiri-shi
accounts department	keiri-ka
advertisement	kōkok
advertising	kōkoku-gyō
to airfreight	eya-hureito
bid	nyūsats
board (of directors)	jūyaku-kai
brochure	pan-huret-to
business card	meishi
businessman	kaisha-in
chairman	kaichō
cheap	yasui
client	okyak-san
company	kaisha
computer	kompyūtā
consumer	shōhi-sha
contract	keiyak
cost	kakak
customer	okyak-san
director	direktā
discount	waribiki
documents	shorui
down payment	atama-kin
engineer	gishi
executive	egzekutib
expensive	takai
exports	yushuts-hin

fax	faks
to import	yunyū suru
imports	yunyū-hin
instalment	bunkats-barai
invoice	seikyū-sho
to invoice	seikyū-sho o tskuru
letter	tegami
letter of credit	shin-yō-jō
loss	sonshits
manager	manējā
manufacture	seizō suru
margin	baibai-saeki
market	shijō
marketing	māket-tin-gu
meeting	kaigi
negotiations	kōshō
offer	mōshide
order	chūmon
to order	chūmon suru
personnel	jinji
price	nedan
product	seihin
production	seisan
profit	rieki
promotion *(publicity)*	sokshin
purchase order	kai-chūmon
sales department	hambai-ka
sales director	hambai-buchō
sales figures	uriage
secretary	hisho
shipment	hunazumi
tax	zeikin
telex	tereks
tender	nyūsats
total	gōkei

My name is ...
Watashi no namae wa ... dess

Here's my card
Meishi o dōzo

Pleased to meet you
Dōzo yoroshku onegai-shi-mass

May I introduce ...?
... o goshōkai itashi-mass

My company is ...
Watashi no kaisha wa ... dess

Our product is selling very well in the UK market
Waga-sha no seihin wa Eikok shijō de hijō ni yoku urete ori-mass

We are looking for partners in Japan
Waga-sha de wa Nihon no pātonā o motomete ori-mass

At our last meeting ...
Sempan no o-uchiawase de wa ...

10%/25%/50%
Jup-pāsento/ni-jū-go-pāsento/go-jup-pāsento

More than ...
... ijō

Less than ...
... ika

We're on schedule
Yotei dōri dess

We're slightly behind schedule
Yotei yori skoshi okurete i-mass

DOING BUSINESS

Please accept our apologies
Mōshi-wake gozai-masen

There are good government grants available
Seihu no hojo ga ari-mass

It's a deal
Kore de yoroshï dess ne

I'll have to check that with my chairman
Kaichō to sōdan shte o-henji shi-mass

I'll get back to you on that
Sono koto wa ato de o-henji shi-mass

Our quote will be with you very shortly
Dekiru dake hayaku mitsumori o sashiage-mass

We'll send it by telex
Terek-ksu itashi-mass

We'll send them airfreight
Eya-hureito de okurasete itadaki-mass

It's a pleasure to do business with you
Otak to torihiki deki-mashte ureshku omoi-mass

We look forward to a mutually beneficial business relationship
Dōzo yoroshku onegai-itashi-mass

RESTAURANT

Japan offers a wealth of eating and drinking places with an amazing variety of cuisines. Many restaurants specialize in a certain type of food, so check before you go in. Menus with prices are often displayed in the window together with very realistic plastic or wax replicas of the food on offer, enabling you to point to what you want to order.

In traditional Japanese-style restaurants you will have to remove your shoes and sit on floor cushions. If you are in a group you can reserve an *ozashki*, a private dining room. Chopsticks are usually used for Oriental food, but knives and forks are always available on request. Western-style food is also widely available, especially in hotels and big department stores (usually on the top floor). Japanese tea usually comes free, together with *oshibori*, a damp cloth to wipe your hands and face. Set lunches, *teishok* or *ranchi*, are very popular and generally good value for money; special portions are available for children, *okosama ranchi*. For notes on etiquette see the Cross-cultural Notes section. Tipping is usually unnecessary since the bill will include a service charge.

For snacks you'll find plenty of street stalls, snackbars, hamburger and pizza restaurants and fried chicken shops. For drinking there are myriads of coffee shops and bars (though beware hostess bars where huge bills run themselves up in no time at all). In summer many department stores open beer gardens on the roof – Japanese beer comes in several varieties, most of which taste like German lager. The traditional drink of Japan is, of course, *sake*, brewed from fermented rice and often served hot.

USEFUL WORDS AND PHRASES

beer	bīru
bill	okanjō
bottle	bin
bowl	chawan
cake	kēki
chef	kok

chopsticks	hashi
coffee	kōhī
cup	kap
fork	hōk
fried chicken	tori no kara-age
glass	gurass
knife	naif
menu	menyū
milk	miruk
plate	osara
receipt	ryōshū-shō
sandwich	sandoichi
serviette	napkin
snack	keishok
soup	sūp
spoon	spūn
sugar	osatō
table	tēburu
tea *(Japanese)*	ocha
(Western)	kōcha
teaspoon	tispūn
tip	chip
waiter	uētā
waitress	uētoress
water	mizu
(iced)	ohiya
wine	wain
wine list	wain risto

A table for one please
Hitori onegai-shi-mass

A table for two please
Hutari onegai-shi-mass

May I see the menu?
Menyū onegai-shi-mass

Can I see the wine list?
Wain risto onegai-shi-mass

What would you recommend?
Nani ga oishī dess ka?

I'd like ...
Watashi wa ... ga ī dess

Can I have one of those?
Sore o hitotsu onegai-shi-mass

Just a cup of coffee, please
Kōhī ip-pai dake onegai-shi-mass

Waiter/waitress!
Chot-to sumi-masen!

Can we have the bill, please?
Okanjō onegai-shi-mass

I only want a snack
Keishok de īn dess

Is there a set menu?
Teishoku ga ari-mass ka?

I didn't order this
Kore wa chūmon shi-masen deshta

May we have some more ...?
Mot-to ... onegai-shi-mass

The meal was very good, thank you
Gochisō-sama deshta, totemo oish-kat-ta dess

My compliments to the chef!
Kok-san wa ude ga ī dess ne!

PLACES TO EAT

きっさてん・喫茶店	**kiss-saten**	coffee shop
けいしょくきっさ 軽食喫茶	**keishoku-kiss-sa**	coffee shop serving light meals
りょうてい・料亭	**ryōtei**	expensive, quality restaurant
かっぽう・割烹	**kap-pō**	expensive, quality restaurant
のみや・飲み屋	**nomiya**	local bar
いざかや・居酒屋	**izakaya**	local bar
レストラン	**restoran**	restaurant
しょくどう・食堂	**shokudō**	restaurant
りょうりや・料理屋	**ryōriya**	restaurant
こりょうりや 小料理屋	**koryōriya**	small local restaurant
めしや・飯屋	**meshiya**	small local restaurant
スナック	**snak**	snackbar
けいしょく・軽食	**keishok**	snackbar
スナックバー	**snakbā**	snackbar
しょうじんりょうりや 精進料理屋	**shōjin ryōriya**	vegetarian restaurant
しょくじどころ 食事所	**shokujidokoro**	very small local restaurant

STARTERS & SOUPS

ハム	**ham**	ham
オードブル	**ōdoburu**	hors d'oeuvres
おつまみ・お撮み	**otsumami**	Japanese-style appetizer
つきだし・突き出し	**tskidashi**	Japanese-style appetizer
いせえび・伊勢海老	**ise-ebi**	lobster
メロン	**meron**	melon
ミネストローネ	**minestorōne**	minestrone
マッシュルームの ポタージュ	**mashrūm no potaj**	mushroom soup
くるまえび・車海老	**kuruma-ebi**	prawns
スモークサーモン	**smōk sāmon**	smoked salmon
みそしる・味噌汁	**misoshiru**	soup with bean paste
トマトスープ	**tomato sūp**	tomato soup

EGG DISHES

ベーコンエッグ	**bēkon-eg**	bacon and eggs
たまご・卵	**tamago**	egg
めだまやき・目玉焼き	**medama-yaki**	fried eggs
ハムエッグ	**hamu-eg**	ham and eggs
たまごやき・卵焼き	**tamago-yaki**	Japanese-style omelette
オムレツ	**omurets**	omelette
オムライス	**omuraiss**	omelette with rice

| ちゃわんむし
茶碗蒸し | **chawam-mushi** | savoury 'custard' with egg and fish |
| たまごどうふ
卵豆腐 | **tamago-dōhu** | steamed egg and bean curd |

FISH & SUSHI

あわび	**awabi**	abalone
すずき	**suzuki**	bass
ふぐ	**hugu**	blowfish
かつお	**katsuo**	bonito, tunny
うな重	**unajū**	broiled eel on rice
こい	**koi**	carp
並	**nami**	cheaper selection
はまぐり	**hamaguri**	clam
たら	**tara**	cod
たらこ	**tarako**	cod roe
あなご	**anago**	conger eel
かに	**kani**	crab
うなぎ	**unagi**	eel
上	**jō**	expensive selection
うBどE・うな丼	**unadon**	grilled eel on rice
にしん	**nishin**	herring
かずのこ	**kazunoko**	herring roe
あじ	**aji**	horse mackerel

さば	**saba**	mackerel
五目寿司	**gomok-zushi**	mixed 'sushi'
散らし寿司	**chirashi-zushi**	mixed 'sushi' on rice
たこ	**tako**	octopus
おしずし	**oshi-zushi**	Osaka-style 'sushi' cut in squares
かき	**kaki**	oyster
さしみ	**sashimi**	raw fish
すし	**sushi**	raw fish on riceballs
にぎりずし	**nigiri-zushi**	raw fish on riceballs
さけ	**sake**	salmon
いくら	**ikura**	salmon roe
いわし	**iwashi**	sardines
帆立て貝	**hotategai**	scallop
たい	**tai**	sea bream
かっぱまき	**kap-pa-maki**	seasoned rice and cucumber wrapped in seaweed
いなりずし	**inari-zushi**	seasoned rice wrapped in fried bean curd
うに	**uni**	sea urchin
えび	**ebi**	shrimp
のりまき	**nori-maki**	sliced roll of rice, vegetables and fish powder wrapped in seaweed

いか	**ika**	squid
あゆ	**ayu**	sweet smelt
ます	**mass**	trout
まぐろ	**maguro**	tuna
鯨	**kujira**	whale
ぶり	**buri**	yellowtail

MEAT & POULTRY

バーベキュー	**bābekyū**	barbecue
ぎゅうにく・牛肉	**gyūnik**	beef
ビーフ	**bīf**	beef
てっぱんやき 天板焼	**tep-panyaki**	beef and vegetables grilled at the table
ぎゅうしょうがやき 牛生姜焼	**gyūshōgayaki**	beef cooked in soy sauce with ginger
ビフテキ	**bihuteki**	beef steak
にわとり	**niwatori**	chicken
あばらにく・肋肉	**abaranik**	chops
コロッケ	**korok-ke**	croquettes
とんかつ・豚カツ	**tonkats**	deep-fried pork cutlets
カツどん・カツ丼	**katsudon**	deep-fried pork on rice
あひる	**ahiru**	duck
ヒレにく・ヒレ肉	**hirenik**	fillet

やきにく・焼肉	**yakinik**	fried pork marinated in soy sauce
くしやき・串焼	**kushiyaki**	grilled meat on skewers
ハンバーグ	**hambāg**	hamburger
レバー	**rebā**	liver
にく・肉	**nik**	meat
にくだんご・肉団子	**nikudango**	meat-filled dumplings
ほねつき・骨付き	**honetski**	on the bone
ぶたにく・豚肉	**butanik**	pork
ぶたしょうがやき 豚生姜焼	**butashōgayaki**	pork cooked in soy sauce with ginger
うずら	**uzura**	quail
カレーライス	**karēraiss**	rice with curry-flavoured stew
ローストビーフ	**rōstobīf**	roast beef
ローストチキン	**rōsto chikin**	roast chicken
ローストポーク	**rōsto pōk**	roast pork
ソーセージ	**sōsēji**	sausage
サーロイン	**sāroin**	sirloin
やきとり 焼き鳥	**yakitori**	skewered fowl cooked over a grill
しゃぶしゃぶ	**shabu-shabu**	sliced beef with vegetables boiled at the table

すきやき・すき焼	**skiyaki**	sliced beef with vegetables cooked at the table
スペアリブ	**speyarib**	spare ribs
すずめ	**suzume**	sparrow
ステーキ	**stēki**	steak

RICE DISHES

…どんぶり・丼	**… domburi**	bowl of rice with something on top
うなぎどんぶり	**unagi domburi**	'domburi' with broiled eel
おやこどんぶり・親子丼	**oyako domburi**	'domburi' with chicken and egg
てんどん・天丼	**tendon**	'domburi' with deep-fried shrimps
たまごどんぶり・卵丼	**tamago domburi**	'domburi' with onions cooked in egg
ちゅうかどんぶり 中華丼	**chuka domburi**	'domburi' with pork and vegetables
にくどん・肉丼	**nikudon**	'domburi' with sliced beef
カツどん・カツ丼	**katsudon**	'domburi' with deep-fried breaded pork cutlet
チャーハン	**chāhan**	fried rice
ごはん・御飯	**gohan**	rice

ライス	**raiss**	rice
かめめし・釜飯	**kamameshi**	rice steamed in fish bouillon with pieces of meat, fish and vegetables
チキンライス	**chikin raiss**	rice with chicken
おにぎり・	**onigiri**	rice balls wrapped in seaweed

VEGETABLES, SEASONINGS & SALADS

アスパラ	**aspara**	asparagus
なす	**nass**	aubergine
竹の子	**takenoko**	bamboo shoots
とうふ	**tōhu**	bean curd
豆	**mame**	beans
おひたし	**ohitashi**	boiled spinach with seasoning
キャベツ	**kyabets**	cabbage
にんじん	**ninjin**	carrots
きゅうり	**kyūri**	cucumber
みそ	**miso**	fermented soybean paste
なっとう	**nat-tō**	fermented soybeans
油揚げ	**abura-age**	fried bean curd
しょうが	**shōga**	ginger
ピーマン	**pīman**	green pepper

67

まつたけ	**mats-take**	Japanese mushrooms
のり	**nori**	kind of seaweed
レタス	**retass**	lettuce
マヨネーズ	**mayonēz**	mayonnaise
マッシュルーム	**mashrūm**	mushrooms
きのこ	**kinoko**	mushrooms (*general term*)
からし	**karashi**	mustard
あぶら・油	**abura**	oil
玉ねぎ	**tamanegi**	onion
ポテト	**poteto**	potatoes
ポテトサラダ	**poteto-sarada**	potato salad
サラダ	**sarada**	salad
塩	**shio**	salt
からい・辛い	**karai**	hot, spicy
しょうゆ・醤油	**shōyu**	soy sauce
大豆	**daizu**	soybeans
ほうれん草	**hōrensō**	spinach
おさとう・お砂糖	**osatō**	sugar
あまい・甘い	**amai**	sweet
コーン	**kōn**	sweetcorn
トマト	**tomato**	tomato
野菜	**yasai**	vegetables
す・酢	**su**	vinegar

| たくあん | **takuan** | yellow radish pickles |

FRUIT & NUTS

バナナ	**banana**	banana
さくらんぼ・桜ん坊	**sakurambo**	cherries
くり・栗	**kuri**	chestnuts
ココナッツ	**kokonats**	coconut
くだもの・果物	**kudamono**	fruit
フルーツ	**huruts**	fruit
グレープフルーツ	**gurēp-hurūts**	grapefruit
レモン	**remon**	lemon
メロン	**meron**	melon
オレンジ	**orenji**	orange
もも・桃	**momo**	peach
かき・柿	**kaki**	persimmon
みかん・蜜柑	**mikan**	tangerine
くるみ・胡桃	**kurumi**	walnuts
すいか・西瓜	**suika**	watermelon

DESSERTS

アップルパイ	**ap-puru pai**	apple pie
ケーキ	**kēki**	cake
チーズケーキ	**chīz-kēki**	cheesecake

MENU READER

チョコレート	**chokorēto**	chocolate
シュークリーム	**shūkurīm**	cream puff
クレープ	**kurēp**	crêpe
うじごおり・宇治氷	**uji gōri**	crushed ice with green tea syrup
氷メロン	**kōri meron**	crushed ice with melon syrup
デザート	**dezāto**	dessert
ドーナッツ	**dōnats**	doughnut
みつまめ・蜜豆	**mitsumame**	gelatin cubes and sweet beans with pieces of fruit
アイスクリーム	**aiskurīm**	ice cream
ゼリー	**zerī**	jelly
パイナップル	**painap-puru**	pineapple
パインヨーグルト	**pa-in yōguruto**	pineapple yoghurt
きいちご	**kīchigo**	raspberry
おもち・お餅	**omochi**	rice cakes
おせんべい	**osembei**	rice crackers
まんじゅう・饅頭	**manjū**	rice-flour cakes with bean jam
シャーベット	**shābet-to**	sherbet
ショートケーキ	**shōto kēki**	sponge-cake with strawberries
ようかん・羊かん	**yōkan**	soft, sweet bean paste

スフレ	**suhure**	soufflé
カステラ	**kastera**	sponge cake
いちご・苺	**ichigo**	strawberries
ストロベリー アイスクリーム	**storoberī aiskurīm**	strawberry ice cream
おしるこ・お汁粉	**oshiruko**	sweet bean soup with rice cake
プリン	**purin**	vanilla egg custard with brown sugar
バニラアイスクリーム	**banira aiskurīm**	vanilla ice cream
クリームあんみつ	**kurīmu am-mits**	vanilla ice cream on gelatin cubes, served with sweet beans and fruit
ヨーグルト	**yōguruto**	yoghurt

NOODLE DISHES

ラーメン・拉麺	**rāmen**	Chinese noodles
チャーシューメン	**chāshūmen**	Chinese noodles in pork broth
チャンポン	**champon**	Chinese noodles in salted broth with vegetables
カントンメン・広東麺	**kantom-men**	Chinese noodles in salted pork-flavoured soup with vegetables
そば・蕎麦	**soba**	long, brownish buckwheat noodles

うどん・饂飩	**udon**	long, thick, white, wheatflour noodles
そうめん・素麺	**sōmen**	long, thin, white, wheatflour noodles
ワンタンメン・饂飩麺	**wantam-men**	noodle-like squares containing ground pork and leeks, served in soup with noodles
やきそば・焼そば	**yaki soba**	noodles fried on griddle with small pieces of vegetable
てんぷらそば 天麩羅蕎麦	**tempura soba**	noodles in fish broth with deep-fried shrimps
つきみそば・月見蕎麦	**tskimi soba**	noodles in fish broth with fried egg on top
にくなんばん・肉南蛮	**niku namban**	noodles in fish broth with pork or beef
かけそば・掛蕎麦	**kake soba**	noodles in fish broth
きつねうどん・狐饂飩	**kitsune udon**	noodles in fish broth with bean curd
ちからうどん・力饂飩	**chikara udon**	noodles in fish broth with rice cake
もやしそば・萌そば	**moyashi soba**	noodles in pork broth with bean sprouts
もりそば・盛り蕎麦	**mori soba**	noodles served cold, to be dipped into sweetened soy sauce

みそラーメン・ 味噌ラーメン	**miso rāmen**	noodles and pork in bean paste broth
ごもくそば・ 五目そば	**gomok soba**	'soba' in broth in pieces of vegetable and meat

JAPANESE-STYLE SET MEALS

定食	**teishok**	set meal with rice, soup, pickles and main dish
ひがわりていしょく 日変り定食	**higawari teishok**	'teishok' of the day
てんぷらていしょく 天麩羅定食	**tempura teishok**	'teishok' with deep-fried prawns as the main dish
やきにくていしょく 焼肉定食	**yakiniku teishok**	'teishok' with grilled meat as the main dish
とんかつていしょく 豚カツ定食	**tonkats teishok**	'teishok' with pork as the main dish
さしみていしょく 刺身定食	**sashimi teishok**	'teishok' with raw fish as the main dish
おひるのていしょく 御昼の定食	**ohiru no teishok**	lunchtime 'teishok'
べんとう・弁当	**bentō**	boxed lunch (*sold at railway stations*)

SNACKS

パン	**pan**	bread
バター	**batā**	butter

チーズロール	**chīzurōru**	cheese roll
フライドチキン	**huraido chikin**	fried chicken
ハムサンド	**hamusando**	ham sandwich
ジャム	**jam**	jam
ランチ	**ranchi**	lunch
マーマレード	**māmarēdo**	marmalade
ピザ	**piza**	pizza
サンドイッチ	**sandoich**	sandwich
スパゲッティ	**spaget-ti**	spaghetti
トースト	**tōsto**	toast

CHINESE MEALS

すぶた・酢豚	**subuta**	a kind of sweet and sour pork
マーボーどうふ マーボー豆腐	**mābo-dōhu**	bean curd in spicy soup mixture
ちゅうかりょうり 中華料理	**Chūka ryōri**	Chinese food
はるまき・春巻	**harumaki**	egg roll, deep-fried
ギョーザ・餃子	**gyōza**	fried dumplings stuffed with minced pork
くらげのすのもの 海月の酢物	**kurage no sunomono**	sliced parboiled jellyfish

| シューマイ・焼売 | **shūmai** | small steamed balls of pork in thin Chinese pastry |

CULINARY CATEGORIES & METHODS OF PREPARATION

のみもの・飲み物	**nomimono**	beverages
ろばたやき・炉端焼	**robatayaki**	charcoal-grilled fish and vegetables
お菓子	**okashi**	confectionery
ちゅうかりょうり 中華料理	**Chūka ryōri**	Chinese-style cuisine
むしもの・蒸し物	**mushimono**	steamed foods
しょうじんりょうり 精進料理	**shōjin ryōri**	vegetarian cuisine
すのもの・酢の物	**sunomono**	vinegared foods
せいようりょうり 西洋料理	**seiyō ryōri**	Western-style cuisine
つけもの・漬け物	**tskemono**	pickled foods
とりりょうり・鳥料理	**tori ryōri**	poultry dishes
きょうどりょうり 郷土料理	**kyōdo ryōri**	regional specialities
ごはんもの・御飯物	**goham-mono**	rice dishes
にもの・煮物	**nimono**	simmered foods
しるもの・汁物	**shirumono**	soups
なべもの・鍋物	**nabemono**	food cooked in a pot at the table

やきもの・焼物	**yakimono**	grilled or broiled foods
かいせきりょうり 懐石料理	**kaiseki ryōri**	Japanese haute cuisine
にほんりょうり 日本料理	**Nihon ryōri**	Japanese-style cuisine
めんるい・麺類	**menrui**	noodle dishes
かっぽう・割烹	**kap-pō**	customer-requested Japanese-style cordon bleu dishes
あげもの・揚げ物	**agemono**	deep-fried foods
てんぷら・天麩羅	**tempura**	deep-fried seafood and vegetables
あえもの・和え物	**aemono**	dressed foods (salads)

DRINKS

ビール	**bīru**	beer
紅茶	**kōcha**	black tea
ココア	**kokoa**	cocoa
コーヒー	**kōhī**	coffee
コーラー	**kōrā**	cola
しょうちゅう・焼酎	**shōchū**	distilled rice spirit
なまビール・生ビール	**nama bīru**	draught beer
ソーダー水	**sōdā sui**	sweet, green soda pop
お茶	**ocha**	Japanese tea
レモンティ	**remon tī**	lemon tea

ミルク	**miruk**	milk
ぎゅうにゅう・牛乳	**gyūnyū**	milk
ミルクセーキ	**miruk sēki**	milkshake
ミネラル ウオーター	**mineraru uōtā**	mineral water
オレンジ ジュース	**orenji jūss**	orange juice
オレンジスカッシュ	**orenji skash**	orange squash
パイン ジュース	**pa-in jūss**	pineapple juice
さけ・酒	**sake**	rice wine
にほんしゅ・日本酒	**nihonshu**	rice wine
サイダー	**saidā**	soda pop
ミルクティ	**miruk tī**	tea with milk
トマト ジュース	**tomato jūss**	tomato juice
トニック ウオーター	**tonik uōtā**	tonic
ウイスキー	**uiskī**	whisky
オン・ザ・ロック	**onzarok**	whisky on the rocks
みずわり	**mizuwari**	whisky with water
ワイン	**wain**	wine
ぶどうしゅ・葡萄酒	**budōshu**	wine

FESTIVAL FOOD

やきいも・焼き芋	**yaki-imo**	baked potato
わたがし・綿菓子	**watagashi**	candy floss
いかやき・烏賊焼	**ikayaki**	charcoal-grilled squid

たこやき・たこ焼	**takoyaki**	griddle-fried octopus
おでん・お田	**oden**	hotchpotch of fish and vegetable boiled in fish broth
あまぐり・甘栗	**amaguri**	roasted chestnuts
とうもろこし・玉蜀黍	**tōmorokoshi**	roasted corn on the cob
おこのみやき お好み焼	**okonomiyaki**	seasoned pancake
たこせんべい 蛸煎餅	**tako sembei**	shrimp-flavoured pink crackers

SHOPPING

A country *par excellence* for shopping, Japan abounds in shops of all sorts – including the ubiquitous souvenir shop. Shops generally open at 10 in the morning and stay open until late in the evening (8 or 9pm), although department stores are usually closed after 6pm. Japanese shops usually close for one day during the week, although many of them will be open on a Sunday. If something is needed urgently then a major railway station is often the place to head for. When you enter a shop, assistants will often call out (and often quite loudly) a word of welcome, *irash-shai-mase!* They can rarely be expected to speak English, though writing down an English word on a piece of paper will often help.

USEFUL WORDS AND PHRASES

audio equipment	ōdio seihin
baker	pan-ya
boutique	butik
butcher	niku-ya
bookshop	hon-ya
to buy	kau
cake shop	keiki-ya
cheap	yasui
chemist	ksuri-ya
department store	depāto
fashion	fash-shon
fishmonger	sakana-ya
florist	hana-ya
grocer	shoku-ryō hinten
ironmonger	kanamono-ya
ladies' wear	hujin huku uriba
menswear	shinshi huku uriba
newsagent	shimbun-ya
receipt	ryōshū-sho

SHOPPING

record shop	rekōdo-ya
sale	sēru
shoe shop	kutsu-ya
shop	mise
to go shopping	kaimono ni ik
souvenir shop	omiyage-ten
special offer	tokubets kakak
to spend	okane o tskau
stationer	bumbōgu-ya
supermarket	sūpā
tailor	shtate-ya
till	reji
toyshop	omocha-ya
travel agent	ryokō-gaisha

I'd like ...
... onegai-shi-mass

Do you have ...?
... ari-mass ka?

How much is this?
Ikura dess ka?

Where is the ... department?
... uriba wa doko dess ka?

Do you have any more of these?
Kō iu no wa mada ari-mass ka?

I'd like to change this please
Kore o tori-kaete kure-masen ka?

Have you anything cheaper?
Mō skoshi yasui no ga ari-mass ka?

Have you anything larger?
Mō skoshi ōki no ga ari-mass ka?

Have you anything smaller?
Mō skoshi chisai no ga ari-mass ka?

Does it come in other colours?
Hoka no iro mo ari-mass ka?

Could you wrap it for me?
Tsutsunde kure-masen ka?

Can I have a receipt?
Ryōshū-shō kure-masen ka?

Can I have a bag please?
Hukuro kure-masen ka?

Can I try it (them) on?
Kite mite mo ī dess ka?

Where do I pay?
Doko de harat-tara ī dess ka?

Can I have a refund?
Okane o kaeshte kure-masen ka?

I'm just looking
Mite-iru dake dess

I'll come back later
Ato de ki-mass

THINGS YOU'LL HEAR

Irash-shai-mase!
Welcome!

Nanika osagashi dess ka?
Are you being served?

Komakai okane ga gozai-mass ka?
Have you any smaller money?

Mōshi-wake gozai-masen ga ima kirashte ori-mass
I'm sorry we're out of stock

Kore dake shka gozai-masen
This is all we have

Hoka ni nanika go-iri-yō dess ka?
Will there be anything else?

Chūmon itashi-mashō ka?
Shall we order it for you?

Omochi-kaeri ni nari-mass ka, otodoke shi-mashō ka?
Will you take it with you or shall we send it?

TYPES OF SHOP

骨董店	**kot-tō-ten**	antique/curiosity shop
パン屋	**pan-ya**	baker
本屋	**hon-ya**	bookshop
書店	**shoten**	bookshop
両替所	**ryōgaejo**	bureau de change
肉屋	**niku-ya**	butcher's

ケーキ屋	**kēki-ya**	cake shop
カメラ屋	**kamera-ya**	camera shop
せともの屋	**setomono-ya**	china shop
お菓子屋	**okashi-ya**	confectioner's
デパート	**depāto**	department store
クリーニング店	**kurīnin-gu-ten**	dry cleaner's
電気屋	**denki-ya**	electrical goods shop
魚屋	**sakana-ya**	fishmonger
花屋	**hana-ya**	florist
果物屋	**kudamono-ya**	fruiterer
八百屋	**yao-ya**	greengrocer's
食料品店	**shokuryō-hin-ten**	grocer's
金物屋	**kanamono-ya**	ironmonger's
売店	**baiten**	kiosk
コインランドリー	**koin-randorii**	launderette
市場	**ichiba**	market
楽器店	**gak-ki-ten**	musical instrument shop
酒屋	**saka-ya**	off-licence
めがね（店）	**megane(-ten)**	optician
質屋	**shchi-ya**	pawnbroker's

→

薬局	**yak-kyok**	pharmacy
写真屋	**shashin-ya**	photography shop
レコード店	**rekōdo-ten**	record shop
みやげ店	**miyage-ten**	souvenir shop
スポーツ用品店	**spōts-yōhin-ten**	sports shop
文房具屋	**bumbōgu-ya**	stationer's
旅行会社	**ryokō-gaisha**	travel agency

THINGS YOU'LL SEE

バーゲン	**bāgen**	bargain
大売リ出し	**ō-uri-dashi**	big bargain sale
会計	**kaikei**	cashier
本日休業	**honjits kyūgyō**	closed today
割引	**waribiki**	discount
民芸品	**mingei-hin**	folk crafts
定価	**teika**	list price
名物	**meibuts**	local speciality
営業中	**eigyō-chū**	open for business
売切	**urikire**	sold out
円	**en**	yen

AT THE HAIRDRESSER

Hairdressing salons by and large reflect those you find in the West, and the hairdressing vocabulary has drawn heavily on English. The Japanese service is typically more extensive, however, with extras like tea or an extended massage offered at no extra charge. Prices are not low, so no tip is required. Barber shops, *rihats-ten*, generally close on Mondays while ladies' hairdressers, *bi-yō-in*, usually close on Tuesdays. (Note also that the first syllable of the word *bi-yō-in* should be given its full value – the slightly shorter word *byōin* means 'hospital'!).

USEFUL WORDS AND PHRASES

appointment	yoyak
beard	hige
blond	burondo
brush	burash
comb	kushi
conditioner	rinss
curlers	kārā
curling tongs	heya-airon
curly	maki-ge
dark	kurop-poi
fringe	hurinj
gel	jeru
hair	kami
haircut	sampats
hairdresser	
(beauty salon)	bi-yō-in
(for men)	rihats-ten
hairdryer	doraiyā
highlights	hairaito
long	nagai
moustache	kuchi-hige

AT THE HAIRDRESSER

parting	wakeme
perm	pāma
shampoo	shampū
to shave	hige o soru
shaving foam	hige-sori yō sek-ken
short	mijikai
styling mousse	stairin-gu mūss
wavy	uēb-shta

I'd like to make an appointment
Yoyak shtain dess

Just a trim please
Skoshi dake kit-te kudasai

Not too much off
Amari kiranaide kudasai

A bit more off here please
Koko, mō skoshi kit-te kudasai

I'd like a cut and blow-dry
Kat-to to burō-dorai onegai-shi-mass

I'd like a perm
Pāma kakete kudasai

I'd like highlights
Hairaito shte kudasai

THINGS YOU'LL HEAR

Dono yō ni nasai-mass ka?
How would you like it?

Kore de yoroshī dess ka?
Is that short enough?

Rinss nasai-mass ka?
Would you like any conditioner?

THINGS YOU'LL SEE

理髪店	**rihats-ten**	barber shop
床屋	**tokoya**	barber shop
美容院	**biyōin**	beauty parlour
ビューティサロン	**byūti-saron**	beauty salon
脱色	**dash-shok**	bleach
色	**iro**	colour
カット	**kat-to**	cut
調髪	**chōhats**	hair cutting
洗髪	**sempats**	hair washing
マニキュア	**manikyua**	manicure
マッサージ	**mass-sāji**	massage
パーマ	**pāma**	perm
ヘアセット	**hea-set-to**	set
シャンプーとセット	**shampū to set-to**	shampoo and set

POST OFFICES AND BANKS

Japan can boast a full and efficient postal system. Post offices display
the $\bar{T}$ symbol and are open from 9 to 5 (except Sundays), although
these hours can be shortened from 9 to 3 for the post office's banking
services such as the encashment of international money orders. Letter
boxes are reddish-orange and in the cities have two slots, the one on
the left being for airmail, special delivery etc. Many smaller post offices
are not equipped to handle overseas packages - these can be sent from
larger post offices where customs declaration forms can also be
completed. There is a 24-hour post office near Tokyo station.

Banks in Japan are open from 9 to 3 Monday to Friday and from
9 to 12 on Saturday. All banks close on Sundays (with the exception
of one at Tokyo's Narita International Airport which stays open 24
hours a day all year round).

Remember that you'll get a better rate for traveller's cheques than
for cash.

Credit cards are widely used, but the use of personal cheques is rare.

USEFUL WORDS AND PHRASES

airmail	kōkū-bin
bank	ginkō
banknote	osats
to change	ryōgae suru
cheque	kogit-te
collection	shūshū
counter	madoguchi
customs form	zeikan-shinkoku-yōshi
delivery	haitats
deposit	yokin
exchange rate	kawase-rēto
form	yōshi
international money order	gaikoku-kawase
letter	tegami

letter box	posto
list of postage rates	yūbim-buts ryōkin-hyō
mail	yūbim-buts
package, parcel	kozutsumi
post	yūbim-buts
postal order	yūbin-kawase
postcard	ehagaki
postcode	yūbim-bangō
poste-restante	kyoku-dome yūbin
postman	yūbin-ya-san
post office	yūbin-kyok
pound sterling	pondo
registered letter	kakitome
stamp	kit-te
surface mail	huna-bin
telegram	dempō
traveller's cheque	toraberāz chek

How much is a letter to ...?
... e no tegami wa ikura dess ka?

How much is a postcard to ...?
... e no ehagaki wa ikura dess ka?

I would like three 20-yen stamps
Nijū-en kit-te o sam-mai onegai-shi-mass

I want to register this letter
Kakitome de onegai-shi-mass

I want to send this parcel to ...
Kono kozutsumi o ... e okuritain dess

I want to send this to England
Kore o Igiriss ni okuritain dess

89

How long does the post to ... take?
... e no yūbin wa dono kurai kakari-mass ka?

Where can I post this?
Kore wa doko de dase-mass ka?

Is there any mail for me?
Tegami ga kite i-mass ka?

I'd like to send a telegram
Dempō uchitain dess

This is to go airmail
Kōkū-bin de onegai-shi-mass

I'd like to change this into yen
Kore o en ni kaete kure-masen ka?

Can I cash these traveller's cheques?
Kono toraberāz chek-ku o genkin ni shte kure-masen ka?

What is the exchange rate for the pound?
Pondo no kawase-rēto wa ikura dess ka?

THINGS YOU'LL HEAR

Paspōto, omochi dess ka?
Can I see your passport please?

Mōshi-wake gozai-masen ga ... wa okotowari shte ori-mass
I'm afraid we don't accept ...

THINGS YOU'LL SEE

住所	**jūsho**	address
あて名	**atena**	addressee
航空書簡	**kōkū shokan**	aerogramme
航空便	**kōkūbin**	airmail
銀行	**ginkō**	bank
記念切手	**kinen kit-te**	commemorative stamp
窓口	**mado-guchi**	counter
税関申告用紙	**zeikan-shinkok-yōshi**	customs declaration form
税関告知書	**zeikan kok-chi-sho**	customs declaration form
速達	**sok-tats**	express mail
外国為替	**gaikoku kawase**	foreign exchange
外国人登録証明書	**gaikokujin tōrok shōmei-sho**	foreign resident's ID card
用紙	**yōshi**	form
身分証明書	**mibun shōmei-sho**	ID card
手紙	**tegami**	letter
為替	**kawase**	money order
地方	**chihō**	out of town mail

→

外国向け	**gaikoku-muke**	overseas mail
小包	**kozutsumi**	parcel
郵便局	**yūbin-kyok**	post office
〒	**yūbin-kyok no māk**	post office symbol
郵便貯金	**yūbin chokin**	post office savings
留置	**tome-oki**	poste restante
印刷物	**insats-buts**	printed matter
現金書留封筒	**genkin kakitome hūtō**	registered cash envelope
書留	**kaki-tome**	registered mail
往復はがき	**ōhuku-hagaki**	return-paid postcard
船便	**hunabin**	sea mail
切手	**kit-te**	stamp
普通便	**hutsū-bin**	surface mail
電報	**dempō**	telegram
アメリカ向け	**Amerika-muke**	to America
イギリス向け	**Igiriss-muke**	to England
都区内	**to-ku nai**	to other parts of Tokyo
他府県	**ta-hu ken**	to other prefectures
円	**en**	yen

TELEPHONING

Public telephones in Japan can be found on the street, in railway stations and coffee shops. A ¥10 coin provides a 3 minute local call. The procedure is as follows: lift the receiver, insert the money, dial the number. The ringing tone consists of a one-second tone followed by two seconds of silence; the engaged tone consists of alternating half-seconds of tone and silence.

The colours of Japanese public telephones are intended to be more than merely decorative and indicate actual differences in function:

● the stocky red phone and the blue phone are for local calls limited to three minutes (not extendable).

● the tall red phone, on the other hand, will accept additional ¥10 coins to extend the call (up to five extra coins can be inserted before dialling).

● the colour pink indicates that the phone is of the stocky red phone type but that it is privately owned (e.g. by a coffee shop); the public may use it by inserting a ¥10 coin.

● the yellow phone takes ¥100 coins and is suitable for long-distance calls; it can, of course, be used for local calls, but change is not given if the ¥100 coin inserted is not all used up.

For emergency calls dial 110 for the police and 119 for an ambulance or the fire brigade. Yellow and blue phones provide this service free of charge. International calls are best made from a private telephone and may be placed through an English-speaking international operator (dial 0051), though this can be very expensive. The code for Britain from Japan is 001-44 (followed by the STD code without the initial 0). The code for the USA is 001-1. Direct dialling overseas is not as widely available as it is in the UK.

To say a phone number just use the ordinary numerals. You can use *no* after the third digit and *ban* (which means 'number') at the end. So 'Tokyo 123-4567' is *Tōkyō ichi-ni-san-no yon-go-roku-nana-ban*.

USEFUL WORDS AND PHRASES

call   denwa

TELEPHONING

to call	denwa suru
code	kyokuban
crossed line	konsen
to dial	daiyaru suru
dialling tone	daiyaru-tōn
emergency	kinkyū
enquiries	an-nai
extension	nai-sen
international call	koksai denwa
number	denwa bangō
operator	kōkan-shu
pay-phone	kōshū denwa
receiver	juwaki
reverse charge call	sempō-barai
telephone	denwa
telephone box	kōshū denwa
telephone directory	denwa-chō
wrong number	machigai bangō

Where is the nearest phone box?
Moyori no kōshū denwa wa doko dess ka?

Is there a telephone directory?
Denwa-chō ga ari-mass ka?

Do you have change for the telephone?
Denwa yō no komakai okane ga ari-mass ka?

I would like the directory for ...
... no denwa-chō onegai-shi-mass

Can I call abroad from here?
Koko kara koksai denwa ga deki-mass ka?

How much is a call to ...?
... e no denwa-ryō wa ikura dess ka?

I would like to reverse the charges
Sempō-barai de onegai-shi-mass

I would like a number in ...
... no bangō o shirabete kure-masen ka?

Hello, this is ... speaking
Moshi-moshi, kochira wa ... dess

Is that ...?
Sochira wa ... dess ka?

Speaking
Hai, sō dess

I would like to speak to ...
... onegai-shi-mass

Extension ... please
Naisen no ... onegai-shi-mass

Please tell him ... called
Kare ni ... ga denwa shta to otstae kudasai-masen ka?

Ask him to call me back please
O denwa kudasaru yō ni otstae itadake-masen ka?

My number is ...
Watashi no denwa bangō wa ... dess

Do you know where he is?
Kare go doko ni irash-sharu ka gozonji dess ka?

When will he be back?
Itsu okaeri ni nari-mass ka?

Could you leave him a message?
Dengon o otstae itadake-masen ka?

TELEPHONING

I'll ring back later
Ato de odenwa shi-mass

Sorry, wrong number
Sumi-masen, machigai denwa dess

REPLIES YOU MAY BE GIVEN

Donata o oyobi dess ka?
Who would you like to speak to?

Denwa bangō ga machigat-te i-mass yo
You've got the wrong number

Donata-sama dess ka?
Who's speaking?

Moshi-moshi
Hello

Odenwa bangō wa namban deshō ka?
What is your number?

Mōshi-wake gozai-masen ga gai-shuts chū dess
Sorry, he's not in

... ji ni modori-mass
He'll be back at ... o'clock

Ashta mō ichido odenwa itadake-masen ka?
Please call again tomorrow

Odenwa ga at-ta to otstae itashi-mass
I'll tell him you called

Odenwa dess
There's a call for you

Henji ga ari-masen
There's no answer

Ohanash chū dess
The line's engaged

Odenwa ga koshō dess
The phone is out of order

THINGS YOU'LL SEE

電電公社	**N.T.T.**	abbreviation of the Japan Public Telegraph & Telephone Company
電話料金	**denwa ryōkin**	call charge
電話代	**denwa-dai**	call charge
代表	**daihyō**	central switchboard
電話帳	**denwa-chō**	directory
非常電話	**hijō denwa**	emergency telephone
内線	**naisen**	extension
国際電話	**koksai denwa**	international call

→

日本電信電話公社	**Nihon Denshin Denwa Kaisha**	Japan Public Telegraph & Telephone Ltd.
市内電話	**shinai denwa**	local call
長距離電話	**chōkyori denwa**	long-distance call
交換手	**kōkan-shu**	operator
市外電話	**shigai denwa**	out-of-town call
K.D.D.	**koksai-denshin-denwa**	Overseas Tele-communication Service
公衆電話	**kōshū denwa**	public telephone
電報	**dempō**	telegram
電信	**denshin**	cable
電話	**denwa**	telephone
電話番号	**denwa bangō**	telephone number

HEALTH

Japan is a world leader in medicine and medical care – also in high prices, so proper medical insurance is essential. It would be wise to take your own medical kit with you in case the medicines you are happy with are not available in the same form in Japan (though Western medicines are available in certain places, such as the 'American Pharmacy' in central Tokyo). If possible, carry a data card showing, for instance, your blood group. For minor problems you can always go to a chemist, *yak-kyok*. For more serious problems, advice on doctors and hospitals catering for foreigners can be obtained from your embassy in Tokyo. For real emergencies memorize *isha – hayak!* ('get a doctor – quick!').

USEFUL WORDS AND PHRASES

accident	jiko
AIDS	eidz
ambulance	kyūkyū sha
anaemic	hinkets (no)
appendicitis	mōchō-en
appendix	mōchō
aspirin	aspirin
asthma	zensok
backache	senaka-ita
bandage	hōtai
bite *(by dog)*	inu no kamare-kiz
(by insect)	mush-sasare
bladder	bōkō
blister	mizu-bukure
blood	ketsueki
burn	yakedo
cancer	gan
chemist	yak-kyok
chest	mune
chickenpox	mizu-bōsō

cold *(noun)*	kaze
concussion	shintō
constipation	bempi
corn	uo-no-me
cough	seki
cut	kiri-kiz
dentist	haisha
diabetes	tōnyō-byō
diarrhoea	geri
dizzy	memai
doctor	isha
earache	mimi-ita
fever	nets
filling	jūten
first aid	ōkyū te-ate
flu	ryūkan
fracture	koss-sets
German measles	hūshin
haemorrhage	shuk-kets
hayfever	kahum-byō
headache	zutsū
heart	shinzō
heart attack	shinzō mahi
hospital	byōin
ill	byōki
indigestion	shōka-huryō
injection	chūsha
itchy	kayui
kidney	jinzō
lump	kobu
measles	hashka
migraine	henzutsū
mumps	otahuku-kaze
nausea	hakike
nurse	kangohu
operation	shujuts
optician	megane-ya

pain	itami
penicillin	penishirin
plaster *(sticky)*	bandēdo
plaster of Paris	sek-kō
pneumonia	haien
pregnant	ninshin shte-iru
prescription	shohōsen
rheumatism	ryūmachi
scald *(noun)*	yakedo
scratch	kaki-kiz
smallpox	ten-nen-tō
splinter	toge
sprain	nenza
sting	sasare-kiz
stomach	onaka
temperature *(fever)*	nets
tonsils	hentō-sen
toothache	ha-ita
travel sickness	norimono yoi
ulcer	kaiyō
vaccination	yobō chūsha
to vomit	modoss
whooping cough	hyakunichi-zeki

I have a pain in …
… ga itami-mass

I do not feel well
Kibun ga yoku ari-masen

I feel faint
Hura-hura shi-mass

I feel sick
Hakike ga shi-mass

I feel dizzy
Memai ga shi-mass

It hurts here
Koko ga itami-mass

It's a sharp pain
Surudoku itami-mass

It's a dull pain
Zuki-zuki itami-mass

It hurts all the time
Itsmo itami-mass

It only hurts now and then
Tokidoki itami-mass

It hurts when you touch it
Sawaru to itami-mass

It hurts more at night
Yoru no hō ga mot-to itami-mass

It stings
Sasu yō ni itami-mass

It aches
Itami-mass

I have a temperature
Nets ga ari-mass

I have a sore throat
Nodo ga itami-mass

I normally take ...
Hudan ... o nomi-mass

I'm allergic to ...
... arerugi dess

Have you got anything for ...?
... ni kiku ksuri ga ari-mass ka?

I have lost a filling
Jūten o nakshi-mashta

THINGS YOU'LL HEAR

... jō o nonde kudasai
Take ... pills/tablets at a time

Mizu de
With water

Kande
Chew them

Ichi-nichi ni ik-kai/ni-kai/san-kai
Once/twice/three times a day

Neru mae ni dake
Only when you go to bed

Hudan wa nani o nomi-mass ka?
What do you normally take?

Sumi-masen, sore wa gozai-masen
I'm sorry, we don't have that

THINGS YOU'LL SEE

救急車	**kyūkyūsha**	ambulance

→

血液	**ketsu-eki**	blood
献血	**kenkets**	blood donation
診療所	**shinryō-jo**	clinic
診療	**shinryō**	consultation
診療時間	**shinryō-jikan**	consultation hours
歯医者	**haisha**	dentist
歯科	**shka**	dentistry
…科	**…ka**	… department
医者	**isha**	doctor
耳鼻咽喉科	**jibi-inkōka**	ear, nose and throat department
眼科	**ganka**	eye department
病院	**byōin**	hospital
産婦人科	**sanhujinka**	obstetrics and gynaecology
小児科	**shōnika**	paediatrics
赤十字	**seki jūji**	Red Cross
医院	**īn**	small hospital
外科	**geka**	surgery, operations

MINI-DICTIONARY

In this mini-dictionary you will see that some words are followed by (no) or (na). If a noun is used following such a word then the 'no' or 'na' must be used:

she is pretty kanojo wa kirei dess
she is a pretty girl kanojo wa kirei na josei dess

about: about 16 jūroku kurai
accelerator akseru
accident jiko
accommodation heya
ache itami
adaptor *(electrical)* adaptā
address jūsho
aeroplane hikōki
after ato
after-shave ahutā-shēb-rōshon
again mata
against hantai
air-conditioning eya-kon
air freshener eya-hureshnā
air hostess eya-hostess
airline kōkū-gaisha
airport kūkō
alcohol arukōru
all zembu
   all the streets michi wa zembu
   that's all, thanks arigatō, sore dake dess
almost hotondo
alone hitori de
already mō
always itsmo
am: I am British Igiriss-jin dess
ambulance kyūkyūsha
America Amerika
American *(person)* Amerika-jin
   (adj) Amerika no

and *(with nouns)* to
   (with verbs) soshte
ankle ashkubi
anorak anorak
another *(different)* bets (no)
   (further) mō hitots (no)
anti-freeze hutō-zai
antique shop kot-tō ten
antiseptic bōhu-zai
apartment apāto
aperitif aperichif
appetite shokuyok
apple ringo
application form mōshkomi-sho
appointment yaksok
apricot anz
are: you are very kind anata wa totemo shinsets dess
   we are English watash-tachi wa Igiriss-jin dess
   they are Japanese karera wa Nihon-jin dess
arm ude
art bijuts
art gallery bijuts-kan
artist geijuts-ka
as: as soon as possible dekiru dake hayak
ashtray haizara
Asia Ajia
asleep: he's asleep kare wa

nemut-te i-mass
aspirin aspirin
at: at the post office
  yūbinkyoku de
  at night yoru
  at 3 o'clock sanji ni
attractive miryok-teki
aunt obasan
Australia Ōstoraria
Australian *(person)* Ōstoraria-jin
  (adj) Ōstoraria no
automatic jidō
away: is it far away? tōi dess
  ka?
  go away! at-chi e it-te!
awful hidoi
axe ono
axle shajik

baby akachan
back *(not front)* ushiro
  (of body) senaka
bacon bēkon
  bacon and eggs bēkon-eg
bad warui
baker pan-ya
balcony barukoni
ball bōru
  (dance) butō-kai
ball-point pen bōru-pen
banana banana
band *(musicians)* bando
bandage hōtai
bank ginkō
banknote osats
bar bā
  bar of chocolate itachoko
barber's tokoya
bargain bāgen
basement chika
basin *(sink)* sem-men-ki

basket kago
bath ohuro
  to have a bath ohuro ni hairu
bathing hat sui-ei yō bōshi
bathroom ohuroba
battery denchi
beach hama
beans mame
beard hige
beautiful utskushī
because kara
  because it is too big
  ōki-sugiru kara
bed bed-do
bed linen shīts to makura-kabā
bedroom shinshits
beef gyūnik
beer bīru
before mae ni
beginner shoshin-sha
behind ushiro
beige bēju-iro (no)
bell beru
below shta
belt beruto
beside soba
best ichiban ī
better mot-to ī
between aida ni
bicycle jitensha
big ōki
bikini bikini
bill okanjō
bird tori
birthday tanjōbi
  happy birthday! otanjōbi
  omedetō!
birthday present tanjōbi no
  okurimono
biscuit bisket-to
bite *(verb)* kamu
  (by insect) mush-sasare

bitter *(adj)* nigai
black kuro
blanket mōhu
blind *(cannot see)* mekura
  (on window) buraindo
blister mizu-bukure
blood ketsueki
blouse burauss
boat hune
body karada
boil *(verb: water)* wakass
  (noun: on body) hare-mono
bolt *(on door)* boruto
bone hone
bonnet *(car)* bon-net-to
book *(noun)* hon
  (verb) yoyak suru
booking office kip-pu uriba
boot *(car)* torank
  (footwear) būts
border kok-kyō
boring tsumaranai
born: I was born in ...
  (place) watashi wa ... de
  umare-mashta
  (year) watashi wa ...nen ni
  umare-mashta
both ryōhō
  both of them hutari tomo
  both of us watash-tachi hutari
  both ... and ... ... to ... to
bottle bin
bottle-opener sen-nuki
bottom *(of box, sea)* soko
bowl chawan
box hako
boy otoko no ko
boyfriend bōi-hurendo
bra burajā
bracelet udewa
braces zubon-tsuri
brake *(noun)* burēki

  (verb) burēki o kakeru
brandy burandē
bread pan
breakdown *(car)* koshō
  (nervous) shinkei-suijak
breakfast chōshok
breathe iki o suru
  I can't breathe iki ga
  deki-masen
bridge hashi
briefcase kaban
British *(things)* Igiriss no
  the British Igiriss-jin
brochure panhuret-to
broken kowareta
  (out of order) koshō
  broken leg ashi ga oreta
brooch burōchi
brother *(older)* onisan
  (younger) otōto
brown cha-iro (no)
bruise dabok-shō
brush *(noun)* burash
bucket bakets
Buddha hotoke
Buddhism buk-kyō
Buddhist *(noun)* buk-kyō-to
  (adj) buk-kyō no
building tatemono
bumper bampā
burglar dorobō
burn *(verb)* moyass
  (noun) yakedo
bus bass
business shigoto
bus station bass no eki
busy *(person)* isogashī
  (crowded) konda
but demo
butcher niku-ya
butter batā
button botan

buy kau
by: by the window mado no
   soba
   by Friday kin-yōbi made ni
   by myself jibun de

cabbage kyabets
cable car kēburu kā
café kiss-sa-ten
cake kēki
calculator keisan-ki
call: what's it called? nan to
   i-mass ka?
camera kamera
can (tin) kanzume
   can I have ...? ... o kure-
   masen ka?
Canada Kanada
Canadian (person) Kanada-jin
   (adj) Kanada no
cancer gan
candle rōsok
cap (bottle) huta
   (hat) bōshi
car kuruma
carburettor kyaburetā
card (business) meishi
cardigan kādigan
careful chūi-bukai
   be careful! ki o tskete!
carpet jūtan
carriage (train) kyak-sha
carrot ninjin
carry-cot akachan no kago
case (suitcase) sūts-kēss
cash (money) genkin
   (coins) komaki okane
   to pay cash genkin de harau
cassette kaset-to
cassette player tēpu rekōdā
castle oshiro

cat neko
cave hora-ana
cemetery bochi
centre sentā
certificate shōmei-sho
chair iss
chambermaid meido-san
change (noun: money) otsuri
   (verb) kaeru
character (written) ji
cheap yasui
cheers! kampai!
cheese chīz
chemist (shop) ksuri-ya
cheque kogit-te
cheque book kogit-te chō
cherry sakurambo
chess chess
chest mune
chewing gum chūin-gam
chicken niwatori
child kodomo
children kodomo-tachi
china tōki
China Chūgok
Chinese (person) Chūgoku-jin
   (adj) Chūgoku no
chips poteto-hurai
chocolate chokorēto
   box of chocolates hakoiri
   chokorēto
chop (noun: food) chop
   (to cut) kizamu
chopstick rest hashi-oki
chopsticks hashi
Christian name namae
church kyōkai
cigar hamaki
cigarette tabako
cinema eiga-kan
city toshi
city centre chūshin-gai

class kurass
classical music koten-ongak
clean kirei (na)
clear (obvious) meihak (na)
  (water) sumikit-ta
  is that clear? wakari-mass ka?
clever kashkoi
clock tokei
  (alarm) mezamash-dokei
close (near) chikai
  (stuffy) iki-gurushī
  (verb) shimeru
  the shop is closed mise wa
  shimat-te i-mass
clothes huku
club kurab
  (cards) kurab
coach chō-kyori bass
  (of train) kyak-sha
coach station bass no eki
coat kōto
coathanger han-gā
cockroach gokiburi
coffee kōhī
coin -dama
  100-yen coin hyaku-en-dama
cold (illness) kaze
  (weather) samui
  (food) tsumetai
collar eri
collection (stamps etc) shūshū
colour iro
colour film karā firum
comb (noun) kushi
  (verb) tok
come kuru
  I come from ... watashi wa
  ... no shush-shin dess
  we came last week watash-
  tachi wa senshū ki-mashta
  come here! koko ni ki-nasai!
compartment shashits

complicated hukuzats (na)
computer kompyūtā
concert ongaku-kai
conditioner (hair) rinss
conductor (orchestra) shki-sha
congratulations! omedetō!
constipation bempi
consul ryōji
consulate ryōji-kan
contact lenses kontakto renz
contraceptive hinin-yak
cook (noun) kok
  (verb) ryōri suru
cooking utensils ryōri-dōgu
cool tsumetai
cork koruk
corkscrew koruk-nuki
corner kado
corridor rōka
cosmetics keshō-hin
cost (verb) kakaru
  what does it cost? sore wa
  ikura kakari-mass ka?
cotton momen
cotton wool dash-shimen
cough (noun) seki
country (state) kuni
  (not town) inaka
cousin itoko
crab kani
cramp keiren
crayfish zarigani
cream (for face, food) kurīm
credit card kurejit-to kādo
crisps poteto-chip
crowded konda
cruise kōkai
crutches matsubazue
cry (weep) nak
  (shout) sakebu
cucumber kyūri
cufflinks kahuss botan

cup kap
cupboard todana
curlers kārā
curry karē
curtain kāten
Customs zeikan
cut *(noun)* kiri-kiz
　(verb) kiru

dad otōsan
damp shimet-ta
dance danss
dangerous abunai
dark kurai
daughter musume
day hi *see page 20*
dead shinda
deaf mimi ga tōi
dear *(person)* shtashī
　(expensive) takai
deckchair dek-cheya
deep hukai
deliberately wazato
dentist ha-isha
dentures ireba
deodorant deodoranto
department store depāto
departure shup-pats
develop *(a film)* genzō suru
diamond *(jewel)* daiyamondo
　(cards) daiya
diarrhoea geri
diary *(record of past events)*
　nik-ki
　(weekly planner type) techō
dictionary jisho
die shinu
diesel dīzeru
different chigau
　I'd like a different one bets
　no ga hoshīn dess

difficult muzukashī
dining car shokudō-sha
dining room shokudō
dinner yūshok
directory *(telephone)* denwa-chō
dirty kitanai
disabled karada no hujiyū (na)
distributor *(in car)* haidenki
dive tobikomu
diving board tobikomi-dai
divorced rikonshta
do suru
doctor isha
document shorui
dog inu
doll nin-gyō
dollar doru
door doa
double room *(hotel)* daburu
　(ryokan) hutari-beya
doughnut dōnats
down shta e
drawing pin oshi pin
dress *(noun)* doress
drink *(verb)* nomu
　(noun) nomi-mono
　would you like a drink?
　nomi-mono wa ikaga dess ka?
drinking water nomi-mizu
drive *(verb)* unten-suru
driver unten-shu
driving licence untem-menkyo
drunk yop-parai
dry kawaita
dry cleaner dorai kurīnin-gu-ya
dummy *(for baby)* oshaburi
during: during ... ... no aida ni
dustbin gomibako
duster dastā
duty-free menzei

each *(every)* sorezore
  two hundred yen each
  sorezore nihyaku en dess
early hayai
earrings iyarin-gu
ears mimi
east higashi
easy yasashī
egg tamago
either: **either of them** dochira
  demo
  either ... or ... ... ka ... ka
elastic gomu-himo
  elastic band wagomu
elbow hiji
electric denki no
electricity denki
electronics denshi-kōgak
else: **something else** nanika
  hokano mono
  someone else dareka hokano
  hito
  somewhere else dokoka
  hokano tokoro
embarrassing hazukashī
embassy taish-kan
embroidery shishū
emerald emerarudo
emergency hijō
emperor ten-nō
empty kara
end owari
engaged *(couple)* kon-yak shta
  (telephone) hanash-chū dess
engine *(motor)* enjin
England Igiriss
English Igiriss no
  (language) Eigo
Englishman Igiriss-jin
Englishwoman Igiriss-jin
enlargement *(of photograph)*
  hikinobashi

enough jūbun
entertainment gorak
entrance iriguchi
envelope hūtō
escalator eskarētā
especially tokuni
Europe Yōrop-pa
evening yoru
every *(morning, day etc)* mai-
  (all) subete no
everyone min-na
everything min-na
everywhere doko demo
example rei
  for example tatoeba
excellent saikō
excess baggage chōka-tenimots
exchange *(verb)* kōkan suru
exchange rate kawase sōba
excursion ensok
excuse me! shitsurei shi-mass!
exit deguchi
expensive takai
explain setsmei suru
extension *(telephone)* naisen
  (lengthening) kakchō
eye drops megusuri
eye(s) me

face kao
faint *(unclear)* usui
  (verb) kizets suru
  to feel faint memai ga
  suru
fair *(funfair)* yūenchi
  it's not fair hukōhei dess
false teeth ireba
family kazok
fan *(folding fan)* senss
  (electric) sempūki
  (enthusiast) fan

fan belt fam beruto
far tōi
   how far is it ...? ... wa
   dono kurai tōi dess ka?
Far East Kyoktō
fare ryōkin
farm nōjō
farmer nōka
fashion fash-shon
fast hayai
fat *(of person)* hutot-ta
   (on meat etc) abura
father otōsan
feel *(touch)* sawaru
   I feel hot atsui dess
   I feel like ... ... no yō na ki ga
   shi-mass
felt-tip pen feruto pen
ferry feri
fever nets
fiancé(e) kon-yak-sha
field nohara
fig ichijik
filling *(tooth)* ha no jūten
   (of sandwich etc) nakami
film *(cinema)* eiga
   (camera) firum
filter firutā
finger yubi
fire hi
   (blaze) kaji
fire extinguisher shōkaki
firework hanabi
first saisho (no)
first aid ōkyū teate
first floor ni-kai
fish sakana tsuri
fishing sakana
   to go fishing tsuri ni ik
fishing rod tsuri zao
fishmonger sakana-ya
fizzy tansan no

flag hata
flash *(camera)* hurash
flat *(level)* taira (na)
   (apartment) apāto
flavour aji
flea nomi
flight hikō
flip-flops zōri
flippers hire-ashi
flour komugi-ko
flower hana
flute hurūto
fly *(verb)* tobu
   (insect) hae
fog kiri
folk music minzoku ongak
food tabe-mono
food poisoning shok chūdok
foot *(on body)* ashi
football sak-kā
   (ball) bōru
for: for ... ... no tame ni
   for me watashi no tame ni
   what for? nan no tame ni?
   for a week ish-shūkan
foreigner gaikoku-jin
forest mori
fork hōk
fortnight ni-shūkan
fountain pen man-nen-hits
fourth yombam-me
fracture zashō
free jiyū (na)
   (no cost) muryō
freezer reitō-ko
fridge reizō-ko
friend tomodachi
friendly shtashimi no aru
front: in front of ... ... no mae
   ni
frost shimo
fruit kuda-mono

fruit juice hurūts jūss
fry ageru
frying pan hurai pan
full ip-pai
  I'm full onaka ga ip-pai dess
full board shokuji tski
funny omoshiroi
  (odd) okashī
furniture kagu

garage *(parking)* shako
  (petrol) gasorin stando
  (repairs) garēji
garden niwa
garlic nin-nik
gay *(happy)* yōki (na)
  (homosexual) homo (no)
gear giya
gear lever giya rebā
geisha (girl) geisha
gents *(toilet)* dansei yō toire
get *(fetch)* mot-te kuru
  have you got ...? ... o mot-te
  i-mass ka?
  to get the train densha ni
  noru
  get back: we get back
  tomorrow ashta kaeri-mass
  to get something back
  kaeshte morau
get in *(to car etc)* noru
  (arrive) tsku
get out *(of bus etc)* oriru
get up *(rise)* okiru
gift okurimono
gin jin
girl on-na no ko
girlfriend gāruhurendo
give ageru
glad ureshī
  I'm glad ureshiku omoi-mass

glass garass
  (for drinking) gurass
glasses megane
gloss prints tsuya no aru
  purinto
gloves tebukuro
glue nori
go ik
  I want to go to ... ... e ikitai
  to omoi-mass
goggles suichū-megane
gold kin
good ī
  good! yokat-ta!
goodbye sayonara
government seihu
granddaughter mago-musume
grandfather ojīsan
grandmother obāsan
grandson mago-musko
grapes budō
grass shibahu
Great Britain Igiriss
green midori-iro (no)
grey hai-iro (no)
grill guriru
grocer *(shop)* shoku-ryō hinten
ground floor ik-kai
guarantee *(noun)* hoshō
  (verb) hoshō suru
guide book an-nai-sho
guitar gitā
gun *(rifle)* jū
  (pistol) pistoru

hair kami
haircut *(for man)* sampats
  (for woman) kat-to
hairdresser bi-yō-in
hair dryer doraiyā
hair spray spurē

half hambun
  half an hour hanjikan
  half board chōshok to yūshok
  tski
ham ham
hamburger hambāg
hammer kanazuchi
hand te
handbag handobag
hand brake hando burēki
handkerchief hankachi
handle *(door)* handoru
handsome hansam (na)
hangover hutska-yoi
happy shiawase (na)
harbour minato
hard katai
  (difficult) muzukashī
hard lenses hādo renz
harmony chōwa
hat bōshi
have mots
  I don't have ... ... o mot-te
  i-masen
  can I have ...? ... o kure-
  masen ka?
  have you got ...? ... o mot-te
  i-mass ka?
  I have to go now ima
  ika-nakereba
hayfever kahum-byō
he kare
head atama
headache zutsū
headlights hed-do raito
hear kik
hearing aid hochōki
heart shinzō
heart attack shinzō mahi
heating dambō
heavy omoi
heel kakato

hello! ā!
help *(noun)* enjo
  (verb) taskeru
  help! taskete!
her: it's her kanojo dess
  it's for her kanojo no dess
  give it to her kanojo ni agete
  kudasai
  her book(s) kanojo no hon
  it's hers kanojo no dess
high takai
highway code kōtsū kisok-shū
hill oka
him: it's him kare dess
  it's for him kare no dess
  give it to him kare ni agete
  kudasai
hire kariru
his: his shoe(s) kare no kutsu
  it's his kare no dess
history rekshi
hitch-hike hit-chi-haik
hobby shumi
holiday yasumi
honest shōjiki (na)
honey hachi-mits
honeymoon shinkon-ryokō
horn *(car)* keiteki
horrible osoroshī
hospital byōin
hot atsui
hot water bottle yutampo
hour jikan
house ie
how? dō?
hungry: I'm hungry onaka ga
  suite i-mass
hurry: I'm in a hurry ima
  isoide i-mass
husband shujin
  your husband goshujin

I watashi
ice kōri
ice cream ais-kurim
ice lolly ais-kyandē
if moshi
ignition tenka-sōchi
ill byōki
immediately suguni
impossible hukanō
in: in Japan Nihon ni
  in Japanese Nihongo de
  in my room watashi no heya
  ni
India Indo
Indian *(person)* Indo-jin
  (adj) Indo no
indicator winkā
indigestion shōka-huryō
infection kansen
information jōhō
injection chūsha
injury kega
ink ink
insect mushi
insect repellent mush-sasare
  yobō-yak
insomnia humin-shō
insurance hoken
interesting omoshiroi
interpret tsūyak suru
invitation shōtai
Ireland Airurando
Irish Airurando no
Irishman Airurando-jin
Irishwoman Airurando-jin
iron *(metal)* tets
  (for clothes) airon
ironmonger kanamono-ya
is: he/she/it is ... kare wa/
  kanojo wa/sore wa ... dess
island shima
it sore

itch *(noun)* kayumi
  it itches kayui dess

jacket jaket-to
jacuzzi jikūji
jam jam
Japan Nihon
Japanese *(person)* Nihon-jin
  (adj) Nihon no
  (language) Nihongo
Japanese-style wahū
jazz jaz
jealous shit-to-bukai
jeans jinz
jellyfish kurage
jeweller hōseki-shō
job shigoto
jog *(verb)* jogin-gu suru
  to go for a jog jogin-gu ni
  dekakeru
joke jōdan
journey ryokō
jumper jampā
just: it's just arrived chōdo
  tski-mashta
  I've just got one left hitots
  dake nokot-te i-mass

key kagi
kidney jinzō
kilo kiro
kilometre kiromētoru
kimono kimono
kiss *(noun)* kiss
kitchen daidokoro
knee hiza
knife naihu
knit amu
know: I don't know
  wakari-masen
Korea Kankok

North Korea Kita Chōsen
South Korea Minami Chōsen
Korean *(person)* Kankoku-jin
  (adjective) Kankoku no

label raberu
lace rēss
ladies *(toilet)* hujin-toire
lady hujin
lake mizu-umi
lamb kohitsuji
lamp stando
lampshade stando no kasa
land *(noun)* tochi
  (verb) chakurik suru
language gengo
large ōki
last *(final)* saigo (no)
  last week senshū
  last month sen-gets
  at last! tsui ni!
late: it's getting late mō osoi
  dess
  the bus is late bass wa
  okurete i-mass
laugh warai
launderette koin-randori
laundry *(place)* sentakuya
  (dirty clothes) sentaku-mono
laxative gezai
lazy: he is lazy kare wa
  namake-mono dess
leaf ha
leaflet chirashi
learn narau
leather kawa
leave *(go away)* deru
  (object) nokoss
left *(not right)* hidari
  there's nothing left nanimo
  nokot-te i-masen

left luggage tenimotsu
  azukari-sho
  (locker) rok-kā
leg ashi
lemon remon
lemonade remonēdo
length nagasa
lens renz
less: less than ... ... yori skoshi
lesson jugyō
letter tegami
letterbox yūbim-bako
lettuce retass
library tosho-kan
licence menkyo
life seikats
lift *(in building)* erebētā
  could you give me a lift?
  nosete kure-masen ka?
light *(not heavy)* karui
  (not dark) akarui
lighter raitā
lighter fuel raitā no gass
light meter roshuts-kei
like: I like you anata ga ski dess
  I like swimming sui-ei ga ski
  dess
  I like it ski dess
  I don't like it ski ja ari-masen
  it's like ... ... no yō dess
lime *(fruit)* yuz
lip salve rip-kurim
lipstick kuchi-beni
liqueur rikyūru
list risto
litre rit-toru
litter gomi-kuz
little *(small)* chīsai
  it's a little big skoshi ōkī dess
  just a little hon no skoshi
liver kanzō
lobster ise-ebi

lollipop ais-kyandē
long nagai
  how long does it take? dono
  kurai kakari-mass ka?
lorry torak
lost property wasure-mono
lot: a lot taksan
  not a lot ōku ari-masen
loud: in a loud voice ōgoe de
  (colour) kebakebashi
lounge raunji
love *(noun)* ai
  (verb) ai suru
lover koibito
low hikui
luck un
  good luck! gud-do rak!
luggage tenimots
luggage rack nimots-dana
lunch chūshok

magazine zash-shi
mail *(verb)* yūsō suru
  (noun) yūbim-buts
make tskuru
make-up keshōhin
man hito
manager manējā
map chizu
  a map of Tokyo Tōkyō no
  chizu
margarine māgarin
market ichiba
marmalade māmarēdo
married: he is married kare
  wa kek-kon shte i-mass
martial arts budō
mascara maskara
mat *(straw)* tatami
match *(light)* mat-chi
  (sport) shiai

material *(cloth)* kiji
mattress mat-toress
maybe tabun
me: it's me watashi dess
  it's for me watashi no dess
  give it to me watashi ni
  kudasai
meal shokuji
meat nik
mechanic shūrikō
medicine ksuri
meeting kaigi
melon meron
menu menyū
message mess-sēji
midday shōgo
middle: in the middle man-
  naka ni
midnight mayonaka
milk miruk
mine: it's mine watashi no dess
mineral water mineraru uōtā
minute hun
mirror kagami
mistake machigai
  I made a mistake
  machigai-mashta
monastery shūdō-in
money okane
month *see page 21*
monument kinen-hi
moon tski
moped tansha
more mot-to
morning asa
  in the morning asa
mosaic mozaik
mosquito ka
mother okāsan
motorbike ōtobai
motorboat mōtā-bōto
motorway kōsok-dōro

mountain yama
mouse nezumi
moustache kuchi-hige
mouth kuchi
move ugok
  don't move! ugoka-naide!
  (house) hik-koss
movie eiga
Mr, Mrs, Ms -san *see page 7*
much: not much skoshi
  much better zut-to i dess
mug kap
mum okāsan
museum hakubuts-kan
mushroom kinoko
music on-gak
musical instrument gak-ki
musician on-gaku-ka
mussels mūrugai
mustard karash
my: my key(s) watashi no kagi
mythology shin-wa

nail *(metal)* kugi
  (finger) tsume
nail file nēru-fairu
nail polish nēru-enameru
name namae
nappy omuts
narrow semai
near: near the door doa no
  chikak
  near London Rondon no
  chikak
necessary hitsuyō
necklace nek-kuress
need *(verb)* iru
  I need ... watashi wa ... ga
  iri-mass
  there's no need to go iku
  hitsyō wa ari-masen

needle hari
negative *(photo)* nega
neither: neither of them
  dochira mo ...-masen
  neither ... nor ... ... mo ...
  mo ...-masen
nephew oi
never kesh-shte
new atarashī
news nyūss
newsagent shimbun-ya
newspaper shimbun
New Zealand Nyūjirando
New Zealander *(person)*
  Nyūjirando-jin
next tsugi
  next week rai-shū
  next month rai-gets
nice steki (na)
niece mei
night yoru
nightclub naito-kurab
nightdress nemaki
no *(response)* ie
  I have no money okane wa
  ari-masen
  no sugar osatō nashide
noisy yakamashī
north kita
Northern Ireland Kita
  Airurando
nose hana
not: not today kyō ja ari-masen
  he is not here koko ni i-masen
  not for me mō kek-kō dess
  not that one sore ja ari-masen
notebook nōto
nothing nanimo
novel shōsets
now ima
nowhere dokonimo
number sūji

number plate nambā-purēto
nurse kangohu
nut *(fruit)* kurumi
   (for bolt) nat-to

occasionally tama ni
octopus tako
of no
   the name of the street michi
   no namae
office jimusho
often yok
oil sekiyu
ointment nankō
OK ok-kē
old *(thing)* hurui
   (person) otoshiyori
olive orīb
omelette omurets
on ue
   on the table tēburu no ue ni
   a book on Tokyo Tōkyō ni
   tsuite no hon
one *(numeral)* ichi
   (+ noun) hitots (no)
onion tamanegi
only dake
open *(verb)* akeru
   (adj) aita
opposite: opposite the hotel
   hoteru no hantai-gawa
or soretomo
orange *(colour)* orenji-iro (no)
   (fruit) orenji
orange juice orenj jūss
orchestra ōkestora
ordinary hutsū no
our watash-tachi no
   it's ours watash-tachi no dess
out: he's out kare wa gaishuts
   shte i-mass

outside soto
over *(more than)* ijō
   (above) ue
   over there mukō
overtake oikoss
oyster kaki

Pacific Ocean Taiheiyō
package *(parcel)* kozutsumi
packet pak
   a packet of ... ... hito-hako
pack of cards kādo hito-kumi
padlock nankinjō
page pēji
pain itami
paint *(noun)* penki
pair hutats (no)
   a pair of shoes kutsu iss-sok
Pakistan Pakistan
Pakistani *(person)* Pakistan no
   hito
   (adj) Pakistan no
pale *(face)* kaoiro ga warui
   (colour) usui
pancakes pankēki
paper kami
   (newspaper) shimbun
parcel kozutsumi
pardon? e, nan dess ka?
parents ryōshin
park *(noun)* kōen
   (verb) chūsha suru
party *(celebration)* pātī
   (group) dantai
   (political) seitō
passenger ryokō-sha
passport paspōto
path komichi
pavement hodō
pay harau
peach momo

peanuts pīnats
pear nashi
pearl shinju
peas mame
pedestrian hokō-sha
peg *(clothes)* sentak-basami
pen pen
pencil empits
pencil sharpener empits kezuri
penfriend pemparu
peninsula hantō
penknife chisai naihu
people hitobito
   (nation) kokumin
pepper koshō
   (red/green) piman
peppermints hak-ka-dorop
per ni tski
   per person hitori ni tski
perfect kanzen (na)
perfume kōsui
perhaps tabun
perm pāma
petrol gasorin
petticoat pechikōto
photograph *(noun)* shashin
   (verb) shashin o toru
photographer shashin-ka
phrase book mame-jiten
piano piano
pickpocket suri
picnic pikunik
piece hito-kire
pillow makura
pilot pairot-to
pin pin
pine *(tree)* mats
pineapple painap-puru
pink pink
pipe *(for smoking)* paip
   (for water) suidō-kan
pizza piza

place basho
plant shokubuts
plaster *(for cut)* bansōkō
plastic purass-chik
plastic bag biniru-bukuro
plate sara
platform hōm
play *(theatre)* geki
pleasant kimochi no ī
please *(give me)* onegai-shi-mass
   (please do) dōzo
   please may I take a picture?
   shashin o tot-te mo ī dess ka?
plug *(electrical)* konsento
   (sink) sen
pocket poket-to
poison dok
police keisats
policeman omawari-san
police station keisats-sho
politics seiji
poor mazushī
   (bad quality) shits ga warui
pop music pop
pork butanik
port *(harbour)* minato
porter pōtā
   (railway station) akabō
possible kanō
post *(noun)* posto
   (verb) posto ni ireru
post box posto
postcard ehagaki
poster postā
postman yūbin-ya-san
post office yūbin-kyok
potato jaga-imo
poultry chōrui
pound *(money)* pondo
powder kona
pram uba-guruma
prawn shiba-ebi

(bigger) ise-ebi
prescription shohōsen
pretty *(beautiful)* kirei (na)
　(quite) kanari
priest *(Shintō)* kan-nushi
　(Buddhist) obōsan
　(Christian) bokushi
private kojin (no)
problem mondai
　what's the problem? dō
　shi-mashta ka?
public ōyake
pull hik
puncture pank
purple murasaki
purse saihu
push oss
pushchair uba-guruma
put ok
pyjamas pajama

quality shits
quay hatoba
question shitsmon
queue *(noun)* rets
　(verb) narabu
quick hayai
quiet shizuka (na)
quite *(fairly)* kanari
　(fully) suk-kari

radiator rajiētā
radio rajio
radish daikon
railway tetsdō
rain ame
raincoat reinkōto
raisins hoshi-budō
rare *(uncommon)* mezurashī
　(steak) reya

rat dobu-nezumi
razor blades kamisori no ha
read yomu
reading lamp denki stando
　(small bedside lamp) doksho
　ramp
ready yōi ga deki-mashta
rear lights tēru-ramp
receipt ryōshū-shō
receptionist uketske
record *(music)* rekōdo
　(sporting etc) kirok
record player rekōdo-prēyā
red akai
refreshments nomi-mono
registered letter kakitome-bin
relative shinrui
relax yut-tari suru
religion shūkyō
remember oboete iru
　I don't remember oboete
　i-masen
rent *(verb)* kass
reservation yoyak
rest *(remainder)* sono hoka
　(relaxation) yasumu
restaurant restoran
return *(come back)* kaeru
　(give back) kaess
return ticket ōhuku kip
rice *(uncooked)* kome
　(cooked) gohan
rich *(person)* kanemochi (no)
　(food) shits-koi
right *(correct)* tadashī
　(direction) migi
ring *(to call)* denwa suru
　(wedding etc) yubiwa
ripe jukushta
river kawa
road michi
rock *(stone)* ishi

(music) rok
roll *(bread)* rōru-pan
roof yane
room heya
  (space) basho
rope tsuna
rose bara
round *(circular)* marui
  it's my round watashi no ban
  dess
rowing boat bōto
rubber *(eraser)* keshigom
  (material) gom
rubbish *(refuse)* gomi
  (poor quality) garakta
ruby *(stone)* rubi
rucksack ryuk-sak
rug *(mat)* shkimono
  (blanket) mōfu
ruins haikyo
ruler *(for drawing)* jōgi
rum ram
run *(person)* hashiru
Russia Roshia
Russian *(person)* Roshia-jin
  (adj) Roshia no

sad kanashī
safe anzen (na)
safety pin anzem-pin
sailing boat hansen
salad sarada
salami sarami
sale *(at reduced prices)* sēru
salmon sake
salt oshio
same: the same dress onaji
  doress
  the same people onaji hito
  same again please mō hitots,
  onegai-shi-mass

sand suna
sandals sandaru
sand dunes sakyū
sandwich sandoich
sanitary towels seiri-yō napkin
sauce sōss
saucepan nabe
sauna sauna
sausage sōsēji
say iu
  what did you say? nan to
  ī-mashta ka?
  how do you say ... in
  Japanese? ... wa Nihongo de
  dō ī-mass ka?
scarf skāhu
school gak-kō
scissors hasami
Scotland Skot-torando
Scottish Skot-torando no
screw neji
screwdriver neji-mawashi
scroll maki-mono
sea umi
seafood kaisam-buts
seat seki
seat belt shīto-beruto
second *(adj)* ni-bam-me (no)
  (time) byō
see miru
  I can't see mie-masen
  I see *(understand)* sō dess ka
sell uru
send okuru
separate bets (no)
separated *(from husband etc)*
  wakareta
sellotape ® serotēp
serious *(situation)* jūdai (na)
  (person) majime (na)
serviette napkin
several sū-

sew nū
shampoo shampū
shave *(noun)* hige-sori
  (verb) hige o soru
shaving foam hige-sori-yō
  sek-ken
shawl shōru
she kanojo
sheet shīts
shell kai
sherry sheri
Shinto *(adj)* shintō no
Shintoism shintō
ship hune
shirt shats
shoe laces kutsu-himo
shoe polish kutsu-zumi
shoes kutsu
shop mise
shopping kaimono
  to go shopping kaimono ni ik
short *(object)* mijikai
  (person) se ga hikui
shorts hanzubon
shoulder kata
shower *(bath)* shawā
  (rain) yūdachi
shrimp ebi
shrine jinja
shutter *(camera)* shat-tā
  (window) amado
sick *(ill)* byōki
  I feel sick kimochi ga waruin
  dess
side *(edge)* hashi
  I'm on her side kanojo no
  mikata dess
sidelights saido-raito
sights: the sights of ... ... no
  kembuts
silk kinu
silver *(colour)* gin-iro (no)

  (metal) gin
simple kantan (na)
sing utau
single *(one)* hitots
  (unmarried) dok-shin
single room shinguru
sister *(older)* onēsan
  (younger) imōto
skid *(verb)* suberu
skin cleanser kurenjin-gu-kurīm
skirt skāto
sky sora
sleep *(noun)* suimin
  (verb) nemuru
  to go to sleep neru
sleeping bag ne-bukuro
sleeping pill nemuri-gusuri
slippers surip-pa
slow osoi
small chīsai
smell *(noun)* nioi
  (verb) niou
smile *(noun)* bishō
  (verb) nik-kori warau
smoke *(noun)* kemuri
  (verb) tabako o sū
snack keishok
snow yuki
so: so good totemo ī
  not so much ... sore hodo ...
  ja ari-masen
soaking solution *(for contact
  lenses)* kontakto-yō hozon-eki
socks kutsu-shta
soda water sōda-sui
soft lenses softo-renz
somebody dareka
somehow nantoka-shte
something nanika
sometimes tokidoki
somewhere dokoka
son musko

song uta
soon mō sugu
sorry! gomen-nasai!
  I'm sorry sumi-masen
soup sūp
south minami
South Africa Minami Ahurika
South African (person) Minami
  Ahurika no hito
  (adj) Minami Ahurika no
souvenir omiyage
spade (shovel) ski
  (cards) spēdo
spanner spana
spares yobihin
spark(ing) plug tenka-purag
speak hanass
  do you speak ...? ... o
  hanashi-mass ka?
  I don't speak ... ... wa
  hanashi-masen
speed spīdo
spider kumo
spoon spūn
sprain nenza
spring (mechanical) bane
  (season) haru
stadium stajiam
staircase kaidan
stairs kaidan
stamp kit-te
stapler hoch-kiss
star hoshi
  (film) stā
start shup-pats
  (verb) shup-pats suru
station eki
statue dōzo
steak stēki
steal nusumu
  it's been stolen
  nusumare-mashta

stewardess schūwādess
stockings stok-kin-gu
stomach onaka
stomach ache huku-tsū
stop (verb) tomaru
  (bus stop) bass-tei
  stop! tomare!
storm arashi
strawberry ichigo
stream ogawa
street tōri
string (cord) himo
  (guitar etc) tsuru
student gaksei
stupid bạka
suburbs kōgai
sugar osatō
suit (noun) sūts
  (verb) au
  it suits you anata ni ai-mass
suitcase sūts-kēss
sun taiyō
sunbathe nik-kō-yok
sunburn hiyake
sunglasses sangurass
sunny: it's sunny hi ga dete
  i-mass
suntan hiyake
suntan lotion hiyake rōshon
supermarket sūpā
supplement (for fares) tsuika-kin
surname myōji
sweat (noun) ase
  (verb) ase o kak
sweatshirt undō-sētā
sweet (not sour) amai
  (candy) ame
swimming costume kaisui-gi
swimming pool pūru
swimming trunks kaisui-pants
switch sui-chi

table tēburu
tablet jōzai
Taiwan Taiwan
take toru
  can I take it with me? mot-te
  it-te mo ī dess ka?
  take a picture! shashin o
  tot-te!
  I'll take a taxi takshī de
  iki-mass
take away mochi-kaeri
take-off ririk
talcum powder tarukamu-paudā
talk *(noun)* hanashi
  (verb) hanass
tall takai
tampon tampon
tangerine mikan
tap jaguchi
tapestry tapestorī
taxi takshī
tea *(Western)* kōcha
  (Japanese) ocha
teahouse chamise
team chīm
tea towel hukin
telegram dempō
telephone *(noun)* denwa
  (verb) denwa suru
telephone box denwa boks
telephone call denwa
television terebi
temperature ondo
  (fever) nets
temple otera
tent tento
than yori
thank *(verb)* kansha suru
  thanks arigatō
  thank you dōmo arigatō
that: that bus ano bass

  what's that? are wa nan dess
  ka?
  I think that ... ... to
  omoi-mass
their: their room(s) karera no
  heya
  it's theirs karera no dess
them: it's them karera dess
  it's for them karera no dess
  give it to them karera ni
  age-nasai
then sore kara
there *(near you)* soko
  (over there) asoko
  there is/are ... ... ari-mass
  there isn't/aren't ... ...
  ari-masen
  is there ...? ... ari-mass ka?
thermos flask mahō-bin
these: these things kono mono
  these are mine korera wa
  watashi no dess
they karera
thick atsui
thin usui
thing *(abstract)* koto
  (concrete) mono
think omou
  I think so sō omoi-mass
  I'll think about it kangaete
  mi-mass
third sambam-me
thirsty: I'm thirsty nodo ga
  kawaite i-mass
this: this bus kono bass
  what's this? kore wa nan dess
  ka?
  this is Mr ... kochira wa ...
  -san dess
those: those things sono mono
  those are his sorera wa kare
  no dess

125

throat nodo
throat pastilles nodo no ksuri
through: through Tokyo Tōkyō keiyu
thunderstorm raiu
ticket kip
tie *(noun)* nek-tai
  (verb) musubu
tights taits
time jikan
  what's the time? ima nanji dess ka?
timetable jikok-hyō
tin *(can)* kan
tin opener kan-kiri
tip *(money)* chip
  (end) saki
tired tskareta
  I feel tired tskare-mashta
tissues tish-shū-pēpā
to: to England Igirisu e
  to the station eki e
  to the doctor oisha-san e
toast tōsto
tobacco tabako
today kyō
toe ashi no yubi
together ish-sho ni
toilet otearai
toilet paper toiret-to pēpā
tomato tomato
tomato juice tomato jūss
tomorrow ashta
tongue shta
tonic tonik
tonight kon-ya
too *(also)* mo
  (excessive) -sugiru
tooth ha
toothache: I have toothache ha ga itain dess
toothbrush ha-burash

toothpaste ha-migaki
torch kaichū dentō
tour ryokō
tourist ryokō-sha
towel taoru
tower tawā
town machi
town hall shiyak-sho
toy omocha
track suit undō-gi
tractor toraktā
tradition dentō
traffic kōtsū
traffic jam kōtsū-jūtai
traffic lights shingō
trailer *(for car)* torērā
train densha
translate hon-yak suru
transmission *(for car)* toransmishon
travel agency ryokō-gaisha
traveller's cheque toraberāz-chek
tray obon
tree ki
trousers zubon
try yat-te miru
tunnel ton-neru
tweezers pinset-to
typewriter taipuraitā
tyre taiya

umbrella kasa
uncle ojisan
under shta
underground chikatets
underpants pants
university daigak
until made
unusual mezurashī
up ue

(upwards) ue made
urgent kyū (na)
us: it's us watash-tachi dess
  it's for us watash-tachi no dess
  give it to us watash-tachi ni
  kudasai
use *(noun)* shiyō
  (verb) tskau
  it's no use yaku-ni tachi-masen
useful yaku-ni tats
usual itsmo no
usually itsmo

vacancy *(room)* aki-beya
vacuum cleaner sōjiki
vacuum flask mahō-bin
valley tani
valve ben
vanilla banira
vase kabin
veal ko-ushi no nik
vegetable yasai
vegetarian saishok-shugi-sha
vehicle kuruma
very totemo
  very much totemo
vest chok-ki
view: a good view ī nagame
viewfinder fainda
villa bess-sō
village mura
vinegar su
violin baiorin
visa biza
visit *(noun)* hōmon
  (verb) hōmon suru
visitor hōmon-sha
  (tourist) ryokō-sha
vitamin tablet bitamin-zai
vodka uok-kā
voice koe

wait mats
waiter uētā
  waiter! sumi-masen!
waiting room machi-ai-shits
waitress uētoress
Wales Uēruz
walk *(noun: stroll)* sampo
  (verb) sampo suru
  to go for a walk sampo ni ik
walkman ® uōk-man
wall kabe
wallet saihu
war sensō
wardrobe yōhuku-danss
warm atatakai
was: I was watashi wa ... deshta
  he was kare wa ... deshta
  she was kanojo wa ... deshta
  it was sore wa ... deshta
washing powder sentak-paudā
washing-up liquid shok-ki yō
  senzai
wasp suzume-bachi
watch *(noun)* tokei
  (verb) miru
water mizu
waterfall taki
wave *(noun)* nami
  (verb) te o huru
we watash-tachi
weather tenki
wedding kek-kon-shki
week shū *see page 21*
wellingtons nagaguts
Welsh Uēruz (no)
were: we were watash-tachi wa
  ... deshta
  you were anata wa ... deshta
  (sing. familiar) kimi wa ...
  deshta

they were karera wa ... deshta
west nishi
　the West seiyō
Westerner seiyō-jin
Western-style yōhū
wet nureta
what? nani?
wheel *(of bicycle)* sharin
　(steering) handoru
wheelchair kuruma-iss
when? its?
where? doko?
which? *(of two)* dochira?
　(of more than 2) dore?
whisky uiskī
white shiroi
who? dare?
why? naze?
wide hiroi
wife tsuma
　my wife kanai
　your wife oksan
wind kaze
window mado
windscreen uindo-skrīn
wine budōshu
wine list wain-risto
wing tsubasa
with *(together with)* to ish-sho ni
　I'll go with you anata to ish-sho ni iki-mass
　(using) de
　with a pen pen de
　with sugar osatō iri
without nashide
　without sugar osatō nashide
woman josei
wood mori
wool yōmō
word kotoba

work *(noun)* shigoto
　(verb) hatarak
　it doesn't work ugoki-masen
worse mot-to warui
worst ichiban warui
wrapping paper tsutsumi-gami
wrist te-kubi
write kak
writing paper binsen
wrong: it is wrong machigat-te i-mass

year *see page 21*
yellow kiroi
yen en
yes hai
yesterday kinō
yet mō
　not yet mada
yoghurt yōguruto
you *(sing. polite)* anata
　(sing. familiar) kimi
　(plural polite) anata-gata
　(plural familiar) kimi-tachi
your: your shoe(s) *(polite)* anata no kutsu
　(familiar) kimi no kutsu
yours: is this yours? *(polite)* kore wa anata no dess ka?
　(familiar) kore, kimi no?
youth hostel yūss hosteru

zen zen
zen Buddhism zen-shū
zen garden zendera no niwa
zip chak
zoo dōbutsu-en